# MILITARY PAY, BENEFITS AND RETIREMENT

# MILITARY PAY, BENEFITS AND RETIREMENT

*John V. Lund*
*(Editor)*

**Nova Science Publishers, Inc.**
New York

**Senior Editors:** Susan Boriotti and Donna Dennis
**Coordinating Editor:** Tatiana Shohov
**Office Manager:** Annette Hellinger
**Graphics:** Wanda Serrano and Matt Dallow
**Editorial Production:** Maya Columbus, Alexis Klestov, Vladimir Klestov,
    Matthew Kozlowski and Lorna Loperfido
**Circulation:** Ave Maria Gonzalez, Vera Popovic, Sean Corkery, Raymond Davis,
    Melissa Diaz, Magdalena Nuñez, Marlene Nuñez and Jeannie Pappas
**Communications and Acquisitions:** Serge P. Shohov
**Marketing:** Cathy DeGregory

*Library of Congress Cataloging-in-Publication Data*

Military pay, benefits, and retirement / John V. Lund, ed.
    p.cm.
Includes index
ISBN 1-59033-877-4 (softcover)
1. United States – Armed Forces—Pay, allowances, etc. 2. United States—Recruiting, enlistment, etc. 3. United States—Armed Forces—Appointments and retirements. I. Lund, John, V.
UC74.M553  2004
331.2`81355`00973—dc22
                                2003024221

Copyright © 2004 by Nova Science Publishers, Inc.
    400 Oser Ave, Suite 1600
    Hauppauge, New York 11788-3619
    Tele. 631-231-7269      Fax 631-231-8175
    e-mail: Novascience@earthlink.net
    Web Site: http://www.novapublishers.com

All rights reserved. No part of this book may be reproduced, stored in a retrieval system or transmitted in any form or by any means: electronic, electrostatic, magnetic, tape, mechanical photocopying, recording or otherwise without permission from the publishers.

The publisher has taken reasonable care in the preparation of this book, but makes no expressed or implied warranty of any kind and assumes no responsibility for any errors or omissions. No liability is assumed for incidental or consequential damages in connection with or arising out of information contained in this book. Any parts of this book based on government reports are so indicated and copyright is claimed for those parts to the extent applicable to compilations of such works.

This publication is designed to provide accurate and authoritative information with regard to the subject matter covered herein. It is sold with the clear understanding that the publisher is not engaged in rendering legal or any other professional services. If legal or any other expert assistance is required, the services of a competent person should be sought. FROM A DECLARATION OF PARTICIPANTS JOINTLY ADOPTED BY A COMMITTEE OF THE AMERICAN BAR ASSOCIATION AND A COMMITTEE OF PUBLISHERS.

*Printed in the United States of America*

# CONTENTS

| | | |
|---|---|---|
| **Chapter 1** | Military Pay and Benefits<br>*Robert L. Goldich* | 1 |
| **Chapter 2** | Military Health Care: The Issue of "Promised" Benefits<br>*David F. Burrelli* | 23 |
| **Chapter 3** | Military Medical Care Services<br>*Richard A. Best, Jr.* | 37 |
| **Chapter 4** | Veterans' Pensions: Fact Sheet<br>*Dennis W. Snook and Alice D. Butler* | 57 |
| **Chapter 5** | Military Retirement<br>*Robert L. Goldich* | 61 |
| **Chapter 6** | Military Technicians: The Issue of Mandatory Retirement for Non-Dual Status Technicians<br>*Lawrence Kapp* | 85 |
| **Index** | | 115 |

*Chapter 1*

# MILITARY PAY AND BENEFITS

*Robert L. Goldich*

## INTRODUCTION

In the late 1990s, the military services were facing considerable recruiting and career retention problems. Reasons for these included the end of the Cold War, private-sector job opportunities in the 1990s boom, increasing desire for and availability of a college education, rising living standards that put military housing and lifestyles at a disadvantage, and greater sensitivity among personnel to frequent family separation and overseas rotations.

In responding, Congress was mindful of how low pay had contributed to decreased recruit quality in the late 1970s. It authorized larger pay raises, increased special pays and bonuses, more recruiting resources, and repeal of planned military retired pay reductions for future retirees. In the midst of these efforts, the terrorist attacks of September 11, 2001, took place, providing a sense of national unity and military purpose. Recruiting has since improved substantially. Career retention is difficult to measure, due to (1) the suspended separation and retirement of many personnel since 09/11/01, (2) the Iraq war, and (3) and the virtual impossibility of disaggregating the effects of each of these factors.

Debate continues over what kinds of pay and benefit increases are best for improving recruiting and retention. Of particular interest is the balance between across-the-board pay raises on the one hand, and ones targeted by grade, years of service, and occupational skill, on the other; and between cash compensation on the one hand and improvements in benefits such as housing, health care, and installation services on the other.

The across-the-board increases in military pay discussed each year relate to military **basic pay,** which is the one element of military compensation that all military personnel in the same pay grade and with the same number of years of service receive. However, there are numerous other elements in the total military compensation "package." These other elements are important in determining whether a "pay gap" exists between military and civilian pay that favors civilians, because the numerous different elements of military pay makes it difficult to compare to civilian salaries and other benefits.

Since the early 1990s, in addition to each year's across-the-board raise, most changes in benefits have favored individual members. These include changes in the cash allowance received by personnel not living in military housing; a drastic overhaul of military health care; and repeal of military retired pay cuts first enacted in 1986.

Military personnel last received an across-the-board pay raise on January 1, 2003; all members received at least a 4.1% increase, and some got as much as 6.5%. For January 1, 2004, DOD has proposed a military pay raise averaging 4.1%, ranging between 2.0% and 6.5%; the House version of the FY2004 National Defense Authorization Act (NDAA) approved the DOD pay raise proposal; the Senate version made some comparatively minor changes in the DOD plan. A variety of other increases in various special pays and benefits are making their way through initial stages of the legislative process, in many cases accelerated because of the Iraq war; two were enacted in the FY2003 supplemental appropriations act, and others will be considered in the legislative vehicle of the FY2004 NDAA.

## MOST RECENT DEVELOPMENTS

On May 22, 2003, the House and Senate passed their versions of the FY2004 National Defense Authorization Act. The House approved the Administration's proposal for the FY2004 military pay raise; the Senate approved most of the Administration's pay raise plan with minor changes. Both versions include various special pays and bonuses, some of which had been introduced as separate bills earlier; many are related to the Iraq war and its aftermath.

## BACKGROUND AND ANALYSIS

### 1. Why Did the Adequacy of Active Duty Military Pay Become a Major Issue Beginning in the Late 1990s?

Since the end of the draft in 1972-1973, the "adequacy" of military pay has tended to become an issue for Congress for one or both of two reasons: if it appears that

- the military services are having trouble recruiting enough new personnel, or keeping sufficient career personnel, of requisite quality; or

- the standard of living of career personnel is perceived to be less fair or equitable than that which demographically comparable civilians (in terms of age, education, skills, responsibilities, and similar criteria) can maintain.

The first issue is an economic inevitability on at least some occasions. In the absence of a draft, the services must compete in the labor market for new enlistees, and — a fact often overlooked — have always had to compete in the labor market for more mature individuals to staff the career force. There are always occasions when unemployment is low, and hence recruiting is more difficult, and others when unemployment is high and military service a more attractive alternative. The second situation, while often triggered by the first, is frequently stated in moral or ethical terms. From that viewpoint, even if quantitative indexes of recruiting and retention appear to be satisfactory, it is argued that the crucial character of the military's mission of national defense, and its acceptance of the professional ethic that places survival below mission accomplishment, demands certain levels of compensation.

The last time Congress dealt with inadequate active duty pay levels was in the early 1980s. Problems in recruiting sufficient new enlistees, and retaining enough career personnel of adequate quality, led to what most of those involved with the issue considered a real crisis. Congressional response over the next several years included back-to-back pay raises in 1980 (11.7%) and 1981 (14.3%) that increased basic pay by almost 28%, raised special pays and bonuses, and created (over DOD objections) the new, and immediately highly successful, Montgomery

GI Bill. These factors, coupled with a rise in unemployment in the early 1980s, led to a complete turnaround in recruiting and retention. By the mid-1980s recruit quality was judged to be at unprecedented high levels, recruiters could be selective in taking young men and women, and career force shortages had vanished.

Beginning in the mid-1990s, several new factors caused recruiting and retention problems severe enough to force Congress to once again deal with this issue. Among the factors cited by analysts were (1) a public impression that the end of the Cold War, meant that military service was no longer interesting, relevant, or even available as a career option; (2) the post-Cold War drawdown in active duty military manpower by 40%, which greatly reduced real and perceived enlistment and career retention opportunities; (3) the 1990s economic expansion, which led to the explosive growth of actual and perceived civilian career options; (4) a rise in civilian consumer living standards against which military families measure their own economic success or failure; (5) concerns over increased family separation due to more operations and training away from home, whether "home" was in the United States or in foreign countries; and (6) a decreased propensity for military service among young people for other reasons, such as anti-military parents and educators; skepticism about new missions such as "operations other than war," "peacekeeping," or "peace enforcement"; and the availability of government educational assistance from other sources ("the GI Bill without the GI").

## 2. What Effects Could the September 11, 2001 Terrorist Attacks on the United States, the U.S. Military Response to Them, and the Iraq War That Began on March 19, Have on Military Benefits?

It is not yet clear what effects the ongoing war against terrorism and the more recent Iraq war will have on military pay and benefits. Recruiting and career retention, especially the former, began to improve in FY2000 and have continued their upward trend in FY2001- FY2002. However, it is difficult to disaggregate the precise effects of recruiting and retention initiatives from other war-related policies. The latter include (1) the invoking of "stop-loss" restrictions (authorized by 10 USC 12305, formerly 673c) that prevent military personnel in occupational specialties designated by DOD from separating or retiring from active duty; (2) anticipation of future pay increases in addition to those that have actually taken effect, and (3) the sense of national unity and military purpose that a direct attack on the homeland can produce.

A wide range of possible additional effects on military compensation of the current situation can therefore be postulated, many of them related to future combat operations. Continued popular support for the President, for the war against terrorism, and for the Armed Forces could continue to make recruiting easier and improve career retention, decreasing the requirement for special pays and bonuses and diminishing pressure to increase the annual comparability raise above what the permanent statutory formula provides each year. However, the requirement to pay active duty pay rates to the tens of thousands of reservists brought on active duty will push manpower costs up, as will large-scale overseas deployments. If it is decided that a permanent increase in active duty manpower strengths is required to support long-term anti-terrorism capabilities, then that too will increase total active duty pay costs.

The events of September 11, 2001, contributed to raising both actual and perceived unemployment — attitudes always good for recruiting, if bad for the country as a whole. Such recruiting might be even more popular, in that psychologically, those who join the armed forces, or decide to stay in, would do so to strike at the cause of America's problems. These factors would reduce the need for spending on both bonuses and higher across-the board pay increases, in terms of military pay being competitive. They would not, however, affect countervailing desires that might be felt to provide more liberal pay and benefit increases as a way of showing gratitude to the armed forces. The effects of the war with Iraq on military pay and benefits can be expected to have broadly similar effects. In short, the prospect of combat could be counterbalanced by those attracted to service out of patriotism, anger, and likely adventure. Career personnel who stay in to fulfill their lifetime missions in a time of need, and because of liberal retention bonuses and special pays, could be balanced by those who feel ready to "pass the torch" to younger people and retire rather than face more combat or overseas deployments, regardless of how much money they were offered.

## 3. What Kinds of Increases in Military Pay and Benefits Have Been Considered or Used in the Past?

Many military compensation analysts have strongly criticized across-the-board rather than selective pay raises. They argue that across-the-board increases fail to bring resources to bear where they are most needed. Percentage increases targeted on particular pay grades and number of years of service (often referred to as "pay table reform") and special pays and bonuses targeted on particular occupational skills, they suggest, would maximize the recruiting and retention gains for the compensation dollars spent. Across-the-board increases also affect a variety of other costs; retired pay, for instance, is computed as a percentage of basic pay. (However, there have been proposals to include special pays and bonuses in retired pay calculations, precisely to provide an additional incentive for the recipients to stay in service.)

The services already do a great deal of such targeting, having maintained a large system of special pays and bonuses since the end of conscription almost 30 years ago. Personnel managers report no indication that such targeted compensation has had the deleterious effects on morale and cohesion that some had feared. Across-the-board pay increases, however, are believed by many to have the advantages of simplicity, visibility, and equity. If everyone gets a similar percentage increase, nobody feel, or can claim, that he or she has been left out. It also shows up immediately, in the person's next paycheck, rather than months or years later when a particular individual is next eligible for a lump sum special pay or bonus (some special pays and bonuses are paid monthly or biweekly, as part of regular pay). It appears certain that, as in the past, overall increases in military cash compensation over the next several years will combine both across-the-board and targeted increases. Both of these increases, because of their broad appeal, may well be the most psychologically sound approach in improving recruiting and retention as much as possible. In addition, there is bipartisan support for major increases in Montgomery GI Bill benefits, although these tend to be among the most costly benefit increases being considered.

Recruiting and retention problems are not necessarily solved only by increasing military pay. Many components of the military compensation system that are important to recruiting and retention efforts, especially the latter, do not involve cash pay. These include health care; housing; permanent change of station (PCS) moving costs and policies; exchanges, commissaries, and other retail facilities; and recreational facilities. A wide range of views about existing military personnel management practices suggest that the services' requirements for both new enlistees and career people could be significantly reduced by changing often long-standing and inter-related assignment, promotion, career development, or retirement policies. Survey research also reveals that the sense of patriotism, public service, and *esprit de corps* found in capable and combat-ready armed forces is extremely significant to both new enlistees and career members.

Furthermore, there are always limits to what increased compensation, whether cash or in-kind, can do to help any organization cope with personnel difficulties. Job and career satisfaction; public and elite views of the importance and legitimacy of the military as an institution; unit morale; success in operational deployments and especially in combat – these may well be independent of compensation variables. High "scoring" in these intangibles, especially for a unique organization and culture like the Armed Forces, can and frequently does balance more tangible problems in compensation. However, few analysts believe that recruiting and retention rates can be brought up to service target levels without substantial increases in pay, so long as an economic expansion continues to generate higher-paying job opportunities in the civilian sector. Many long-time observers seem to feel that money alone cannot keep a person in the military for a full career if the person does not like the military culture; they assert that the lifestyle is too demanding and too arduous for most. At the same time, it is argued that people can be driven out of the military if their compensation and living standards are not at least somewhat close to those of their demographic and educational counterparts in civilian life.

## 4. How Are Each Year's Increases in Military Pay Computed?

### *Definitions*

The across-the-board increases in military pay discussed each year relate to military **basic pay**. Basic pay is the one element of military compensation that all military personnel in the same pay grade and with the same number of years of service receive. **Basic allowance for housing**, or **BAH**, is received by military personnel not living in military housing, either family housing or barracks). **Basic allowance for subsistence**, or **BAS**, is the cost of meals. All officers receive the same BAS; enlisted BAS varies, based on the type and place of assignment. A **federal income tax advantage** accrues because the BAH and BAS are not subject to federal income tax.

Basic pay, BAH, BAS, and the federal income tax advantage all comprise what is known as **Regular Military Compensation (RMC)**. RMC is that index of military pay which tends to be used most often in comparing military with civilian compensation; analyzing the standards of living of military personnel; and studying military compensation trends over time, or by service geographical area, or skill area. Basic pay is between 65 and 75% of RMC, depending on individual circumstances. RMC specifically *excludes* all special pays and bonuses, reimbursements, educational assistance, deferred compensation (i.e., an economic valuation of future retired pay), or any kind of attempt to estimate the cash value of non-monetary benefits such as health care or military retail stores.

## *Annual Percentage Increases in Military Basic Pay*

### Military Basic Pay Raises Linked to Federal General Schedule (GS) Civil Service Pay Raises

Permanent law (37 USC 1009) provides that monthly basic pay is to be adjusted upward by the same "overall average percentage increase in the General Schedule [GS] rates of both basic pay and locality pay for [federal] civilian employees," and is to "carry the same effective date." The upward adjustment is based on the GS percentage pay increase that would result from operation of the permanent statutory GS pay raise formula. It need not, therefore, be identical to the actual percentage increase in GS pay, if Congress acts to either (1) authorize a GS pay increase different from that which would result from operation of the permanent formula for a particular fiscal year and/or (2) authorize a different military pay increase that differs from operation of the permanent formula.

### How GS Civil Service Pay Raises Are Computed

The GS formula employed here is that specified in 5 USC 5303(a). It is based on (but is not identical to, as will be discussed below) the increase in the Employment Cost Index (ECI) calculated by the Department of Labor's Bureau of Labor Statistics. The ECI measures annual percentage increases in wages for all private-sector employees, although it can be subdivided to measure increases in specific categories of such employees. The precise ECI increase used for pay purposes is computed by comparing the ECI for the third quarter of the calendar year preceding that in which the pay increase is budgeted with the ECI for the third quarter of the year preceding the latter year. For example, assume the GS civilian pay raise for fiscal and calendar year 2005, under current law to be first paid on January 1, 2005, is being computed. The FY2005 federal budget that includes this pay raise will be debated and enacted in calendar year 2004, beginning with the transmittal of the Administration's FY2005 budget to Congress in early 2004. This latter budget, however, was prepared beginning in the middle of 2003. The pay raise in this budget can only be based on the extent to which the ECI for the third quarter of 2003 had increased over that for the third quarter of 2002. There is thus a lag of approximately 6 months between the end of the ECI increase measuring period and the transmittal of the proposed pay raise based on it to Congress and a lag of 15 months between the end of the ECI measuring period and the actual percentage increase in civil service pay, and hence active duty military pay, on which it is based.

The actual percentage increase in GS pay is not the percentage increase in the ECI over the time frame described. The applicable statute [5 USC 5303(a)] provides that the overall increase in federal GS pay will be 0.5% *less* than the percentage increase in the ECI. The money thus saved is frequently cited as being available to provide larger pay raises to federal civilians in high-cost-of-living metropolitan areas within the United States, although there is no statutory requirement than the "saved" money be used for this purpose. For example, if there is a 5% increase in the ECI from the previous year, and the cost of raising all federal GS pay by 5% would be $5 billion yearly, federal GS civil servants would actually be guaranteed only a pay raise of 4.5%, costing a total of $4.5 billion. The $500 million thus saved could, if the executive branch and/or Congress so desired, be applied to pay for raises higher than 4.5% in high-cost-of-living areas. In this example, military personnel could thus get a 4.5% pay raise. This formula led to the actual pay raises received in 1993 (FY1994), 1994 (FY1995), 1995 (FY1996), 1997 (FY1998), and 1999 (FY2000). [The statute does allow the overall percentage increase to be allocated among the different pay grade and years-of-service categories, subject to various limitations, rather than giving all personnel identical percentage increases. This was in fact done in 2000. See 37 USC 1009(d).]

## Congress Usually Passes a Military Pay Raise Anyway, Despite the Permanent Formula

Despite the existence of this statutory formula, which would operate each year without any further statutory intervention, Congress has legislated a particular percentage increase in military pay every year since 1980, with the exception of 1982, and is in the process of doing so in 2003. The percentage increase in military pay was usually identical to that granted GS civilians during the period 1982-1999 (the exceptions were in 1985 and 1994, when Congress provided larger increases in military pay). However, beginning in 2000, Congress has provided larger increases in military pay each year and may well do so in 2003. Even when the percentage increase has been identical for both military and civilian pay, in most cases Congress has explicitly reiterated the increase in law rather than simply allowing the permanent statutory linkage to operate. Therefore, although Congress may legislate the pay raise percentage, until recently it was a *pro forma* matter, and the operation of the permanent formula remains important in determining what the percentage will actually be.

## Annual Increases in Basic Allowances for Housing (BAH) and Subsistence (BAS)

Housing (37 USC 403) and subsistence (37 USC 402) allowances are paid to all personnel not living in military housing or eating in military facilities or using field rations. Monthly BAH varies by rank, by whether the person has dependents, and, most importantly, by location. Monthly BAS is uniform for all officers regardless of rank or dependents, but BAS for enlisted personnel is computed daily and varies by locations and the kind of eating facilities, military and civilian, deemed available. Annual increases in BAH and BAS are both based on surveys of local housing and national food costs respectively, and thus are not affected by the annual percentage increase in the ECI. (For many years BAH and its predecessors and BAS were subject to the annual percentage increase; this was not changed until the late 1990s.) There have been some proposals in recent weeks, mentioned in the defense trade press, that BAH housing costs be surveyed more frequently than once a year, due to rising housing costs generally. Particular emphasis is placed by supporters of more frequent surveys on fast-rising electricity costs, notably for heating and cooling, being faced by military personnel. In addition, the fact that BAS is a fairly small amount and has long since ceased to bear any real relationship to food and dining costs for individual service-members has led to some calls to merge BAS with basic pay and reduce the complexity of military compensation and the need for BAS computations each year.

## 5. What Have Been the Annual Percentage Increases in Active Duty Military Basic Pay Since 1993 (FY1994)? What Were Each Year's Major Executive and Legislative Branch Proposals and Actions on the Annual Percentage Increase in Military Basic Pay?

The following subsections itemize action on the active duty military basic pay increase going back to 1993 (the FY1994 budget). **Unless otherwise noted, all increases were proposed to be effective on January 1 of the fiscal year indicated. The same is true of discussions of future pay raises.**

### *2003 (FY2004)*

**Statutory formula: 3.7%**

*Administration request*: The FY2004 defense budget request, released on February 3, 2003, proposed an FY2004 military pay raise averaging 4.1%. Depending on rank and years of service, military pay would be increased by a minimum of 2.0% and a maximum of 6.5%. Personnel in pay grade E-1 (new recruits) would get the minimum 2.0% raise, and enlisted members in pay grade E-2, and newly commissioned junior officers in pay grade O-1, would get 3.2%.

Most officers would get 3.7%, and the highest percentage raises, up to the 6.25% figure, would be given to career enlisted personnel in pay grades E-5 through E-9. *House action*. The House version of the FY2004 NDAA, passed May 22, is identical to the Administration proposal. *Senate action*. The Senate version, also passed May 22, would provide military personnel with an average 4.15% pay raise but, unlike the House committee version, would guarantee all personnel at least a 3.7% increase. The Senate version would also modify permanent law to require, after FY2006, that the annual military pay raise be equal to the percentage annual increase in the Employment Cost Index (ECI; see above, under #4, for a description of the ECI), repealing existing permanent law that has the effect of mandating a pay raise equal to the ECI minus 0.5%. Existing temporary law, enacted in 1999 in the FY2000 NDAA, that requires an increase equal to the ECI plus 0.5% in FY2001-FY2006 would not be changed (see below under "Suspension of Statutory Formula during FY2001-FY2006).

## *2002 (FY2003)*

**Statutory formula: 4.1%**

*Administration request*: Minimum 4.1%; average 4.8%; for some mid-level and senior noncommissioned officers, warrant officers, and mid-level commissioned officers, between 5.0% and 6.5%. *Final increase*: identical to the Administration request, embodied, as usual, in the FY2003 National Defense Authorization Act (P.L. 107-314, December 2, 2002; 116 Stat. 2458). The House and Senate had also approved the Administration request.

## *2001 (FY2002)*

**Statutory formula: 4.6%**

*Administration request*: numerous figures for the "Administration request" were mentioned in the pay raise debate, depending on when and which agency produced the figures. In general, however, they all proposed increases of at least 5% and no more than 15% (the latter applying only to a very few individuals), depending on pay grade and years of service. *Final increase*: Eventually, the FY2002 National Defense Authorization Act (Sec. 601, P.L. 107-107, December 28, 2001) endorsed an "Administration request" of between 5 and 10%, depending on pay grade and years of service. These increases are the largest across-the-board percentage raises since that of FY1982, which took effect on October 1, 1981. The latter was a 14.3% across-the-board raise, which followed an 11.7% raise the previous year, FY1981, resulting in a 2-year raise of almost 28%. This was principally in response to the high inflation of the late 1970s.

## *2000 (FY2001)*

**Statutory formula: 3.7% (based on the 1999/FY2000 legislation, above; the original statutory formula would have led to a proposed raise of 2.7%)**

*Administration request*: 3.7%. *Final increase*: The FY2001 National Defense Authorization Act (Section 601, P.L. 106-398, October 30, 2000; 114 Stat. 1654A-1 at A-143) approved the 3.7% figure. In addition, as was the case in the previous year, additional increases averaging 0.4% (based on the size of the across-the-board raise the amount of money used would have funded; the range of additional percentage raises was between 1.0 and 5.5%) were provided to middle-grade officer and enlisted personnel, to be effective July 1, 2001.

## *1999 (FY2000)*

**Statutory formula: 4.8%**

*Administration request*: 4.4% on January 1, 2000, but in addition, on July 1, 2000, a wide range of targeted increases averaging an additional 1.4% (again, based on the size of across-the-board raise the cost of the targeted increases would finance) in mid-level officer and enlisted grades' pay levels. *Final increase*: The FY2000 National Defense Authorization Act (Section 601, P.L. 106-65; October 5, 1999) raised the January 1, 2000 increase to 4.8%, and accepted the July 1, 2000 targeted increases.

## *Suspension of Statutory Formula during FY2001-FY2006*

The FY2000 defense authorization contained a 6-year suspension of the existing statutory formula, which became effective in FY2001. In enacting this suspension, the House version would have required that the full ECI increase (not the ECI less 0.5%) be used in calculating the annual pay raise starting in FY2001 and thereafter. The Senate version would have required that the annual raise be the full ECI **plus** 0.5% (i.e., a full percentage point above what permanent law then read) during FY2001-FY2006. The Senate version prevailed in conference.

## *1998 (FY1999)*

**Statutory formula: 3.1%**

*Administration request*: 3.6%. The House approved 3.6%, or whatever percentage increase was approved for federal GS civilians, whichever was higher. The Senate approved 3.6%. *Final increase*: The FY1999 Strom Thurmond National Defense Authorization Act (Section 601, P.L. 105-261; October 17, 1998; 112 Stat. 1920 at 2036) approved the House alternative, which resulted in a 3.6% military increase, as GS civilians also received 3.6%.

## *1997 (FY1998)*

**Statutory formula: 2.8%**

*Administration request*: 2.8%. *Final increase*: FY1998 National Defense Authorization Act (Section 601, P.L. 105-85, November 18, 1997; 111 Stat. 1629 at 1771): 2.8%.

## *1996 (FY1997)*

**Statutory formula: 2.3%**

*Administration request*: 3.0%. *Final increase*: The House and Senate both approved the higher Administration request of 3.0%, and it was therefore included in the FY1997 National Defense Authorization Act (Section 601, P.L. 104-201, September 23, 1996; 110 Stat. 2422 at 2539).

## *1995 (FY1996)*

**Statutory formula: 2.4%**

*Administration request*: 2.4%. *Final increase*: Congress also approved 2.4% in the FY1996 National Defense Authorization Act (Section 601, P.L. 104-106, February 10, 1996; 110 Stat. 186 at 356).

## *1994 (FY1995)*

**Statutory formula: 2.6%**

*Administration request*: 1.6%. One percent less than the statutory formula. *Final increase*: The FY1995 National Defense Authorization Act (Section 601, P.L. 103-337, October 5, 1994; 108 Stat. 2663 at 2779) authorized the statutory formula figure of 2.6%.

## 1993 (FY1994)

**Statutory formula: 2.2%**

*Administration request*: No increase; military (and civil service) pay would have been frozen in FY1994. The Administration also proposed limiting future civil service – and hence active duty military – pay raises to one percentage point less than that provided by the existing statutory formula. None of these proposals was adopted. *Final increase*: The FY1994 National Defense Authorization Act (Section 601, P.L. 103-160, November 30, 1993, 107 Stat. 1547 at 1677) authorized 2.2%.

## 6. Is There a "Pay Gap" Between Military and Civilian Pay, So That Generally Military Pay Is Less than That of Comparable Civilians? If So, What Is the Extent of the "Gap"?

The allegations of a military-civilian "pay gap" beg several questions:

- How can the existence of a gap be determined and the gap be measured?
- Is there a gap, with civilians or the military being paid more? If so, how much of a gap?
- If there is a gap, does that in itself require action?
- What are the effects of such a gap?

A wide range of studies over the past several decades have compared military and civilian (both federal civil service and private sector) compensation. In general, the markedly different ways in which civilian public and private sector compensation and benefit systems are structured, compared to that of the armed forces, makes it difficult to validate any across the board generalizations about whether there is a "gap" between military and civilian pay. Some advocates for federal civil servants suggest that federal civilian pay lags behind private sector pay, which in turn leads some people, given the linkage between civil service and military pay percentage increases, to infer that military pay lags behind private sector pay. However, because the current statistic used to measure private sector pay, the ECI, measures annual percentage increases and not dollar amounts, no such inference is really possible.

## *Measuring and Confirming a "Gap"*

It is extremely difficult to find a common index or indicator to compare the dollar values of military and civilian compensation. First, military compensation is much more complicated and composed of many more different elements than is civilian compensation. Military cash pay include numerous separate components; some are received by all military personnel and some, such as a wide range of special pays and bonuses, are paid to select groups. One aspect of military pay, the federal income tax advantage that accrues due to housing and meals allowances not being taxable, has a dollar amount that is entirely dependent on each military member's personal tax situation. Which of these should be included in a military-civilian pay comparison? How can some be included at all? Furthermore, total military compensation includes a wide range of non-monetary benefits: the extensive military health care facility network, military retail stores such as commissaries and exchanges; and military recreational facilities such as theaters, gymnasia, hotels, and lodges. Few civilians work in organizations where analogous benefits are provided. Attempts to facilitate a comparison by assigning a cash value to noncash benefits almost always founder on the large number of often arbitrary assumptions that must be made to generate such an estimate.

Second, it is also extremely difficult, for obvious reasons, to establish a solid comparison between military ranks and pay grades on the one hand, and civil service and private sector job titles and pay levels on the other. The range of knowledge and skills, degree of supervision, and scope of professional judgment required of military personnel and civilians performing similar duties in a standard peacetime industrial or office milieu may well be similar. When the same military member's likely job in the field, possibly in combat, is concerned, comparisons become difficult.

Third, generally speaking, with some exceptions, the conditions of military service are frequently much more arduous than those of civilian employment, even in peacetime, for families as well as military personnel themselves. This aspect of military service is sometimes cited as a rationale for military compensation being at a higher level than it otherwise might be. These conditions include frequent moves for which moving allowances never completely reimburse the military member; lengthy family separations, which are not confined to overseas deployments but also result from field training or service at sea even while stationed in the United States; and family disruption resulting from constant changes of occupations and schools by dependents. On the other hand, the military services all mention travel and adventure in exotic places as a positive reason for enlistment and/or a military career, so it may be misleading to automatically assume it is only a liability.

Fourth, comparisons between different sets of compensation statistics, and the use of these comparisons to determine what military pay should be, can yield very different results. Comparing *dollar amounts* of pay received by various military pay grades with the dollar amounts received by comparable federal civil service and private-sector positions (as noted above, in itself a difficult comparison to make) may lead to different conclusions than comparing the *annual increases* in pay for each position. The percentage increase in pay over different time periods – in particular, the percentages that result from picking different base years from which increases or decreases are computed – is more often than not very different. Different indexes with different components can be used to determine compensation changes. The yearly increase in the Consumer Price Index (CPI), which measures the cost of a fixed list of various goods and products at any one time, is used to compute the annual cost-of-living-adjustment (COLA) to military retired pay (and several other federal retirement payments to individuals). The annual Employment Cost Index (ECI) determines not pay levels, but percentage pay increases.

Finally, the level of specificity used in a pay comparison can lead to sharply differing results, especially when the comparison is between private sector and federal pay as a whole, both civil service and military. For instance, all Army colonels may, according to some indexes, be paid roughly as much as federal civil service GS-15s, or as much as private sector managers with certain responsibilities. Thus, those occupational specialties that are highly paid in the private sector – health care, information technology, some other scientific and engineering skills, are examples – are frequently paid considerably less in the military or in the civil service. Other common subcategories for comparison, in addition to occupational skill, include age, gender, years in the labor force, and educational levels.

### *Estimates of a Military-Civilian Pay Gap*

Numerous comparisons of military and civilian compensation in recent years have been cited to illustrate a gap that favors civilian pay levels or refutes the existence of such a gap. Many of these reports lack precision in identifying what aspects of military pay were compared with civilian pay; what indexes were used to make the comparison, or the length of time covered by the comparison. Although it is difficult to generalize, it would appear that most of those estimates which assert that there is a pay gap in favor of higher civilian pay quote a percentage difference of between 7 and 15% in recent years. Most, if not all, of these estimates are across-the-board, comparing all military personnel with all civilian workers in a very broad category.

Some estimates have been made that question the existence of a gap favoring civilians. These tend to compare specific populations of military personnel with equally specific subcategories of civilians, using such criteria as age, occupational skill, and educational level. Analyses of this nature appear to be less common than the across-the-board comparisons, almost certainly because they are much more difficult to do in terms of time, cost, and availability of skilled analysts with the competence to perform them. In 1998, for instance, a Rand Corporation study that broke down military personnel and civilians along these lines asserted that when all of these differing factors were taken into account, there was no pay gap for all enlisted personnel except for senior enlisted members, where the gap was about 3%, and that for officers the gap favoring civilians was about 7%, with some officer subgroups making considerably more money than there civilian counterparts.

In April 2002, in testimony before the Manpower and Personnel Subcommittee of the Senate Armed Services Committee, General Accounting Office (GAO) analysts itemized the components of the military benefit package – i.e., military retirement, health care, Service-member's Group Life Insurance; base recreational facilities, and the like – and compared them with the private sector. It found that the range of benefits available to military personnel was generally comparable to, and in some cases superior to, benefits available in the private sector. The GAO study did not appear to have made dollar-figure comparisons or compared in military non-cash benefits – such as health care, commissaries or exchanges, or annual leave – with similar benefits in the private sector, either by figuring out their dollar worth or by itemizing their exact provisions in great detail.

### *If There is a Pay Gap, Does It Necessarily Matter?*

Some have suggested that the emphasis on the pay gap, whether real or imagined, or if real, how much, is unwarranted and not a good guide to arriving at sound policy. They argue that the key issue is, or should be, not *comparability* of military and civilian compensation, but the *competitiveness* of the former. Absent a draft, the armed forces must compete in the labor market for new enlisted and officer personnel. The career force by definition has always been a "volunteer force," and thus has always had to compete with civilian opportunities, real or perceived. Given these facts of life, it is asked what difference it makes whether military pay is much lower, the same, or higher than that of civilians? If the services are having recruiting difficulties, then pay increases may be required, even if the existing "gap" favors the military. Conversely, if military compensation is lower than equivalent civilian pay, and if the services are doing well in recruiting and retaining sufficient numbers of qualified personnel, then there may be no reason to raise military pay at all.

However, some believe that explicitly basing military compensation on "purely economic" competitiveness with civilian pay could have undesirable consequences: for instance, in a time of economic difficulty, the military might be receiving lower pay than most civilians but still recruiting satisfactorily due to high unemployment. This situation, last existed, to a degree, during the Great Depression of 1929-1941.

## 7. What Recent Changes Have Been Made in Active Duty Military Pay and Benefits (Other Than the Annual Percentage Increase in Basic Pay)?

### *Recent Major Changes in Active Duty Pay and Benefits*

During the late 1990s, several structural changes in active duty military compensation took place, mostly to the benefit of the individual. Three of the most significant are listed below.

### *Complete Restructuring of In-U.S. Housing Allowances*

By 1997, DOD and Congress had completed combining several separate military housing allowances into one, so that all military personnel in the United States not living in military housing have an area tailored housing allowance. This has greatly reduced out-of-pocket housing costs, as DOD continues to budget progressive decreases in those costs as it has over the past several years.

### *Total Overhaul of Military Health Care Obtained from Civilian Sources*

The post-Cold War reduction in the size of the Armed Forces and the closure of many military bases has greatly reduced the size of the military health care establishment and its ability to deliver health care to eligible beneficiaries, particularly military retirees and their families. This has led to large increases in military retiree health care costs and attempts to restrain such costs through administrative and managerial reforms. These initiatives have evolved into the new TRICARE program, which offers beneficiaries a wider range of health care insurance costs and benefits. It is too soon to know if any of these programs will save money or improve health care; as of now, the latter seems more likely than the former.

## *Repeal of the 1986 "Redux" Retirement Cuts*

In late 1999, Congress repealed the Military Retirement Reform Act of 1986 (P.L. 99-348; July 1, 1986), which had made compulsory cuts in the future retired pay of those military personnel who first entered military service on or after August 1, 1986. (These cuts have come to be called the "Redux" system.) Redux had represented a success for those who had argued that the pre-1986 military retirement system, established in the late 1940s, cost too much, had lavish benefits, and contributed to inefficient personnel management. Others had argued that the existing system – particularly, its central feature of allowing career personnel with 20 years of service to retire at any age – was essential to recruiting and maintaining sufficient high-quality career personnel. The 1999 repeal of Redux was thus a success for those who felt that Redux was a major factor in growing retention problems.

## 8. Congressional Action in 2003 on Military Pay and Benefits (Other than the Across-the-Board Pay Raise)

### *FY2003 Emergency Wartime Supplemental Appropriations Bill*

On April 3, 2003, the House and the Senate approved their versions of the FY2003 emergency wartime supplemental appropriations bill. The Senate version (S. 762), has the following military compensation-related features: (1) it increases imminent danger/hazardous duty pay, known colloquially as "combat pay," from $150/month to $225/month; and (2) it increases the military family separation allowance from $100 per month to $200 per month.

### *FY2004 National Defense Authorization Act (NDAA)*

On May 22, 2003, the House and Senate approved their versions of the FY2004 National Defense Authorization Act. Both approved various special pays and bonuses and other elements of military compensation and benefits, some of which had been introduced as separate bills earlier; many are related to the Iraq war and its aftermath. These include the following.

## House and Senate Versions, FY2004 NDAA

- A special pay of up to $1,000 monthly for service-members making very "long or frequent" deployments.
- Increasing the amount of unused leave service-members can carry over from one year to the next from 30 to 120 days.
- A bonus of up to $4,000 to enlisted personnel who agree to serve for at least two years in an occupational specialty critically short of members.

## House Version, FY2004 NDAA

- Authorizing reserve retirees under age 60 (i.e., not yet eligible for reserve retired pay), Selected Reserve personnel, and their dependents to use commissaries on the same unlimited basis as active duty military personnel and their dependents.

## Senate Version, FY2004 NDAA

- Payment of $100 per month to all personnel stationed in South Korea.
- Increasing the death gratuity payable immediately to the survivors of military personnel who die on active duty from $6,000 to $12,000.
- Continuing payment of reserve reenlistment bonuses to reservists who are mobilized.
- Payment of a military Survivor Benefit Plan annuity to the surviving spouse of a reservist not yet eligible for retirement who died during reserve inactive duty training (colloquially often known as "weekend drill).

## Family Separation Allowance and Hostile Fire/Hazardous Duty Pay in the FY2004 NDAA

P.L. 108-11, the FY2003 Emergency Wartime Supplemental Appropriations Act, increased, for FY2003 only, hazardous duty/hostile fire pay from $150 monthly to $225 and the family separation allowance from $100 monthly to $250. The House version of the FY2004 NDAA would continue these higher amounts in FY2004 only for those personnel deployed in and around Afghanistan as part of Operation Enduring Freedom and in and around Iraq as part of Iraqi Freedom. The House version would use the money saved by not making an across-the-board permanent increase in both special pays to fund an increase in active duty military personnel strength of approximately 6,200 troops in FY2004. The Senate version of the FY2004 NDAA would make the increases permanent.

## Long Distance Telephone Subsidy Bill

S. 718 would authorize up to $40 monthly in long distance telephone fees for military personnel directly supporting military operations in Iraq and Afghanistan.

## Military Tax Legislation

### Armed Forces Tax Fairness Act of 2003

Both the House and the Senate have now enacted different versions of the proposed Armed Forces Tax Fairness Act of 2003 in the 108th Congress. Both versions include the following six matters of interest to substantial numbers of military personnel: (1) exemption of the full military death gratuity from income tax, rather than just $3,000 of it; (2) authorization of military personnel to not count periods spent outside the United States in claiming the $250,000 (or $500,000 per couple) capital gains tax exclusion from the sale of real estate; currently, such time spent abroad must be used in determining if the people involved have lived in the residence in question for at least 2 of the preceding 5 years; (3) exclusion from taxation payments made to military home sellers to compensate them for the lowered price of houses in an area where a base has been closed; (4) inclusion of contingency operations in the extended period for which a military member can postpone filing tax returns; currently, the member can postpone the filing only if he or she is in a combat zone; (5) liberalization of the ability of reservists to claim various travel and lodging expenses as unreimbursed business expenses on their tax returns; and (6) clarification of the treatment of certain child care costs for exclusion from taxable income. Both bills also include very specialized tax provisions relating to veterans' organizations, astronauts, and service academy cadets and midshipmen. The Senate bill, however, includes a wide range of other tax provisions that are not related to military personnel that are absent from the House bill. The House version (H.R. 1307) passed March 20, 2003 (422-0; Roll Call No. 76); the Senate (H.R. 1307, as amended), March 27 (97-0, Record Vote No. 110).

### Jobs and Growth Tax Relief Reconciliation Act of 2003 ("Tax Cut Bill")

The above provisions of the different versions of the Armed Forces Tax Fairness Act of 2003 were included in the Senate, but not the House, version of the recent tax cut bill. However, the House prevailed in conference, so none of the provisions were included in the version approved by both houses on May 23, 2003.

## FOR ADDITIONAL READING

*Army Times, Navy Times, Marine Times, Air Force Times*, weekly issues, dated Monday of each week.

Congressional Budget Office. *What Does the Military "Pay Gap" Mean?* June 1999.

Department of Defense. *Morale and Quality of Life Study Issues Document/Briefing Slides and Study Overview*. Located online at the DOD's Web site at [http://www.defenselink.mil/news/Jun2001/d20010621qoli.pdf].

*Uniformed Services Almanac; National Guard Almanac, Reserve Forces Almanac, Retired Military Almanac. 2003 Editions.* Falls Church, VA, Uniformed Services Almanac, Inc., 2003.

*Chapter 2*

# MILITARY HEALTH CARE
# THE ISSUE OF "PROMISED" BENEFITS

*David F. Burrelli*

## INTRODUCTION

In recent years, numerous efforts have been made to increase, or prevent any decrease, of health care benefits and options available to military retirees. Many military retirees and others seeking these increases, or attempting to prevent any decrease in their benefits, often justify their claims based on assertions that the medical care promised to them is no longer available.[1] These retirees say that the relatively large military medical infrastructure that existed during the cold war provided greater access for retirees. They note that as a result of the reduction of the size of the Department of Defense (DOD), fewer medical facilities are available.[2] In certain instances, organizations representing military retirees have alluded to "broken promises." Some individuals have claimed that these benefits

---

[1] About 365,000 elderly retirees and dependents-a thousand a day-will be seen by military doctors this year, Defense Department officials say." Adde, Nick, Medical care access not difficult for all, *Army Times*, February 23, 1998: 22.
[2] Burrelli, David F., and Elizabeth A. Dunstan, *Military Retiree Health Care: Base Closures and Realignments*, CRS Report 95-435, March 28, 1995.

include "free" health care for life, or more liberally, "free care for life in military health care facilities."

Such contentions are not supported by a review of the legislative history of the statutory language related to military health care for retirees and dependents. Nor, with the possible exception of a very few of the literally thousands of different pieces of recruiting literature distributed to prospective recruits and current military members, are these claims supported by written documentation. More recently, a number of bills have been introduced seeking to expand military health care options. In the 106th Congress, at least four of these (H.R. 2966, H.R. 3573, S. 2003 and S. 2013) cite a "promise" or "commitment" as the rationale for provisions that would "restore health care coverage to retired members of the uniformed services."[3]

Although none of these became law, Congress substantially expanded the military retiree health care benefits via the FY2001 National Defense Authorization Act.[4]

## BACKGROUND

Under current law, active duty personnel are entitled to military health care and have a right or claim to this care. Active duty dependents are also entitled to this care, however, this entitlement is limited to space or service availability restrictions. Such an entitlement obligates the military to provide this care (subject to any stated restrictions such as space-availability for active duty dependents). As enforced by the Department of Defense, and interpreted by the courts, retirees and their dependents, while eligible for care on a space- or service-available basis, have no entitlement in statute to such care. In other words, they have no right to military health care and the military services have total discretion in when and under what circumstances retirees and their dependents will get care in military treatment facilities or MTFs. Those dependents and retirees (under age 65) who are unable to get care at MTFs can seek care via civilian providers under DOD's Tricare benefit plan.

---

[3] H.R. 2966, Rep. Shows, October 5, 1999; H.R. 3573, Rep. Shows, February 2, 2000; S. 2003, Sen. Johnson, January 24, 2000; and, S. 2013, Sen. McCain, January 27, 2000. These bills are discussed later in this report. Other legislation seeking to expand military health care benefits include: S. 1335, Sen. Ashcroft, July 1, 1999; H.R. 955, Rep. Collins, March 29, 1999; H.R. 1413, April 14, 1999; H.R. 1547, Rep. Thornberry, April 22, 1999; H.R. 1067, Rep. Thornberry, March 3, 1999; S. 915, Sen. Gramm, April 29, 1999; and, S. 350, Sen. Hutchison, February 3, 1999.

[4] P.L. 106-398, Oct. 30, 2000.

Tricare is the name of the health benefit plan for all military beneficiaries. Tricare is composed of three types of coverage: Prime, Extra and Standard. Tricare Prime is comparable to a Health Maintenance Organization (HMO) using the MTF as the base of health care services. Tricare Extra is similar to a Preferred Provider Organization or PPO. Finally, Tricare Standard is a fee-for-service plan (formerly known as the Civilian Health and Medical Program of the Uniformed Services, (CHAMPUS[5])). Active duty personnel and their dependents are automatically enrolled in Tricare Prime. Retirees (under age 65) and their dependents must enroll in Tricare Prime or seek care via Tricare Extra or Standard. At age 65, retirees lose eligibility for Tricare and become eligible for Medicare benefits. Thus, military service provides lifetime care from a number of government-sponsored or reimbursable sources.[6]

With the passage of the FY2001 National Defense Authorization Act, beginning in October 2001, eligible military retirees over age 64 will be allowed to participate in Tricare provided that they are enrolled in Medicare Part B.

## "THE PROMISE"

The creation of health care benefits and the rules and regulations pertaining to these benefit are matters for Congress. Under the Constitution, Congress has the authority

> To make Rules for the Government and Regulation of the land and naval Forces.[7]

Without explicit authorization from Congress, such benefits can not be created nor conferred by the military or others. A search of the relevant literature shows that at no time did Congress authorize rules and regulations providing "free health care for life at military facilities" for military retirees. Some have asserted that prior to 1956, the lack of legal language to the contrary allowed the military to be contractually obliged to provide "promised" care. However, under our system of government, the military does not have the constitutional authority to create such a contractual obligation. The courts (as discussed below on pages 5, 6, and 7) have held that only Congress has such authority under the Constitution.

---

[5] P.L. 89-614, 80 Stat. 862, September 30, 1966.

[6] This general benefit structure is not new, nor has its consideration by Congress been a recent phenomenon. For example, see U.S. Congress. House. Committee on Armed Services, CHAMPUS and Military Health Care, Subcommittee 2, Hearings, 93rd Cong., 2nd Sess., HASC No. 93-70, October 8, 1974. Interestingly, claims of "free health care for life" did not surface in these hearings.

[7] U.S. Constitution, Art. 1, Sec. 8, cl. 14.

The history of military health care shows that care provided to active duty members was originally paid for by the members as far back as 1799.[8] In that year, Congress enacted legislation for the military establishment to care for the "regimental sick" as well as an act for the "relief of sick and disabled seamen."[9] Later changes provided permissive care to dependents and, later still, to retirees and their dependents. However, at no time were military retirees provided an entitlement to care. In 1956, Congress put the permissive nature of this benefit into law:

> ... a member or former member of a uniformed service who is entitled to retired or retainer pay, or equivalent pay may, upon request, be given medical and dental care in any facility of any uniformed service, subject to the availability of space and facilities and the capabilities of the medical and dental staff.[10] [Emphasis added.]

In 1966, Congress created Medicare which was designed to provide health care for people over age 65 as well as certain disabled individuals. A problem arose in that military personnel tended to retire at a relatively younger age (in most cases, early- to mid-40s) and could be without guaranteed access to health care until age 65. In other words, these retirees were not entitled to military health care and were too young to participate in Medicare. In an effort to address this inability to gain access, as well as provide for those active duty dependents who could not gain access to military medical facilities, Congress created the Civilian Health and Medical Program of the Uniformed Services (CHAMPUS). Modeled after the Blue Cross/Blue Shield high option, CHAMPUS was a fee-for-service benefit. Although it required no premiums, CHAMPUS did require cost sharing on the part of the beneficiary. Thus, CHAMPUS was not free, nor did it relate to care from MTFs. (As noted above, CHAMPUS later became part of Tricare.)

Numerous claims have been made concerning "promises" to military personnel and retirees with regard to health care benefits. Many appear to believe that they were "promised free health care for life at military facilities." Efforts to locate written authoritative documentation of such "promises" have not been successful. However, some military recruiting literature does make general statements about health care. As an example, a recruiting brochure cited by The Retired Officers Association states:

---

[8] U.S. Congress. House. Committee on Armed Services, Subcommittee No. 2, CHAMPUS and Military Health Care, 93d Cong., 2d Sess., December 20, 1974: 6.
[9] 1 Stat. 721 and 1 Stat. 729, March 2, 1799, respectively.
[10] 10 United States Code, sec. 1074(b).

## Military Health Care

> Health care is provided to you and your family members while you are in the Army, and for the rest of your life if you serve a minimum of 20 years of Federal service to earn your retirement.[11]

This language, of course, does not mention "free" health care. Nor does it mention that such care is to be provided via the military health services system and/or in military facilities. This advertised statement is correct in that military retirees do receive their promised lifetime benefits via MTFs (including space- or service-available care in retirement), Tricare and Medicare - all earned as a result of their federal military service.

The same source quotes a 1991 CRS report as stating that "the 'free health care for life' promise was functionally true and had been used to good advantage for recruiting and retention"[12] The report is much more nuanced, and developed the analysis more deeply than this.[13] It noted that the 1956 legislation did not authorize a legal entitlement for care to be provided to retirees and their dependents, but that the retiree and dependent population, in proportion to the available space in military health care facilities, was so low that as a practical matter, such care was usually available. It also observed that this de facto availability was, without question, a useful tool for recruiters. The end result appears to be that, regardless of the lack of statutory entitlement, many active duty personnel and their dependents, and retirees and their dependents, erroneously came to believe that they were guaranteed free health care in military facilities for life.

Other sources have noted that such promises, whether or not actually made, are groundless. For example, in responding to questions from Congress concerning what benefits were promised, Rear Admiral Harold M. Koenig, Deputy Assistant Secretary of Defense for Health Affairs, sought to clarify a statement made by Vice Admiral Hagen concerning these benefits. Rear Admiral Koenig stated in 1993 that:

> There is a problem here of interpretation. [Vice Admiral Donald Hagen, Medical Corps Surgeon General, U.S. Navy] said medical care for life. That is true. We have a medical care program for the life of our beneficiaries, and it is pretty well defined in the law. That easily gets interpreted to, or reinterpreted into, free medical care for the rest of your life. That is a pretty easy transition for people to make in their thinking, and it is pervasive. We

---

[11] Army brochure cited and reproduced in The Retired Officers Association Magazine, April 1996.
[12] The Retired Officers Association, April 1996. This CRS report was also similarly represented in Roberts, C.R., "Veterans Call It The Big Lie," The American Legion, October 1995: 18. The article is based on exerts from The News Tribune, Tacoma, WA, by the same author.
[13] Best, Dick, Memo to Congress, Promises of Lifetime Medical Care, April 21, 1997.

spend an incredible amount of effort trying to reeducate people that that is not their benefit.[14]

According to the Department of Defense, "[a]s thus formulated, medical care for retirees in military medical facilities has always been, and to this day remains, a privilege, not an absolute right, as has been assumed by many."[15]

The federal courts have repeatedly held that such claims of a "promise" have no legal standing. In late 1997, a U.S. District Court dismissed a lawsuit by retirees against the U.S. seeking "free health care" from the military. According to the court:

> The court must reject plaintiffs' contention that [10 United States Code sec. 1074(b)] confers authority on the military branches to guarantee free lifetime medical care to retirees and their dependents. First, plaintiffs cite to no regulation under sec. 1074(b) guaranteeing such care, but only cite to recruiting materials that make general representations as to eligibility for continued health care for retirees and their dependents. Even if the military departments had promulgated regulations under sec.1074(b) that make an unequivocal promise of lifetime medical care for retirees and their dependents, the language of sec. 1074(b) itself is clearly conditional. Any regulations purporting to guarantee free and unconditional lifetime health care to retirees and their dependents would be inconsistent with the statute and therefore invalid. *Larionoff*, 431 U.S. at 873 n.13 ("A regulation which ... operates to create a rule out of harmony with the statute ... is a mere nullity.") (citing *Manhatten General Equip. Co. V. Commissioner*, 297 U.S. 129, 134 (1936)).
>
> Furthermore, under sec. 1074(b), "a retired member of a uniformed service is not entitled to medical care as a matter of right," *Lord v. United States*, 2 Cl. Ct. 749, 756 (1983), and "retired personnel who fail to receive such care cannot successfully maintain an action for money damages based on such failure." *Id.* At 757; see also Watt v. United States, 246 F. Supp. 386, 388 (E.D.N.Y. 1965) ("furnishing [medical care in a military facility] to a retired soldier is discretionary, not mandatory"). Because the law states that retirees are not entitled to health care as a matter of right, the representations upon which plaintiffs rely are to no effect.[16]

---

[14] U.S. Congress. House. Committee on Armed Services, National Defense Authorization Act for Fiscal Year 1994, H.R. 2401, Hearings, 103rd Cong., 1st Sess., H.Rept. 103-13, April 27, 28, May 10, 11, and 13, 1993: 505.
[15] U.S. Department of Defense, Office of the Secretary of Defense, Military Compensation Background Papers, Fifth Edition, September 1996: 609.
[16] Coalition of Retired Military Veterans, et al. V. United States of America, U.S. Dist. of South Carolina, C.A.#2:96-3822-23, Dec. 10, 1997: 11-12.

With respect to the contention that recruiters and others allegedly made "promises of free care for life," and that such "promises" must be honored by the government, the court notes:

> Federal officials who by act or word generate expectations in the people they employ, and then disappoint them, do not *ipso facto* create a contract liability running from the Federal Government to the employee .... [17]

In a separate case (Schism and Reinlie v. U.S.), another federal judge found military "retirees 65 and older do not have a binding contract with the Pentagon that guarantees them free health care for life at military hospitals."[18]

In 1999, a federal appeals court stated:

> Nothing in these regulations provided for unconditional lifetime free medical care or authorized recruiters to promise such care as an inducement to joining or continuing in the armed forces. While the Retirees argue that the above mentioned section 4132.1 gave those of them who served as officers in the Navy and Marine Corps the right to free unconditional medical care, we cannot agree. The [1922 Manual of the Medical Department of the United States Navy] Manual provided guidelines for the Navy's Medical Department, but did not create any right in such officers to the free unconditional lifetime medical care they claim. It related only to hospital care, not the broader services that these Retirees seek, and covered only the period when it was in effect. In any event, in view of the general pattern of the military regulations that provides medical care to retirees only when facilities and personnel were available, we decline to read into the creation of such an enduring and broad right to unconditional free lifetime medical care.
>
> In sum, we conclude that the Retirees have not shown that they have a right to the health care they say was "taken" by the government. Since the basic premise of their claim fails, their taking claim necessarily also fails.[19]

On December 8, 1999, the Coalition of Retired Military Veterans appealed their case to the Supreme Court.[20]

---

[17] Coalition v. U.S.: 15-16.
[18] Adde, Nick, Judge: lifetime care is no guarantee, Army Times, Sept. 21, 1998: 10. An appeal in this case is anticipated. Schism and Reinlie v. U.S. No. #:96cv349/RV United States District Court, N.D. Florida, June 10, 1997.
[19] Sebastain v. United States, 185 F.3d 1368, 1372 (Fed. Cir. 1999). An appeal of this decision is pending.
[20] Adde, Nick, Retirees head to Supreme Court, The Times, January 10, 2000: 14.

On February 8, 2001, the U.S. Court of Appeals for the Federal Circuit reversed the lower court ruling (Schism and Reinlie v. U.S.) declaring "... the government breached its implied-in-fact contract with retirees when it failed to provide them with health care benefits."[21]

The appeals court reversed the district court decision and remanded the case for a determination of damages. Despite various claims, this finding applied only to the two named plaintiffs (and not to all military retirees), and no determination of damages was made. (Some have erroneously reported that the ruling "would have required the government to pay to three million retirees, widows and dependents up to $10,000 apiece."[22]) On June 13, 2001, the Appeals Court vacated the judgment, withdrew its opinion, and agreed to rehear the appeal en banc. As stated "[t]he court has determined to rehear this case en banc to resolve the question of whether the promises of free lifetime care made to and accepted by Plaintiffs-Appellants should be afforded binding effect."[23]

On November 18, 2002, the U.S. Court of Appeals (voting 9-4) stated:

> In the end, because no actual authority existed for the recruiters' promises of full free lifetime medical care, the plaintiffs cannot show a valid implied-in-fact contract. Thus, the plaintiffs, claim must fail as a matter of law.[24]

The claim of "free" or "promised" care is often reported in the media or by lobbying groups. Some media sources have contradicted the notion of free health care for life.[25]

Conversely, others appear to accept or support the existence of such "promises." Although these sources have no legal authority to effect such claims, their repetition of these so-called promises may serve to create or reinforce the notion of the existence of such "promises."[26]

---

[21] Schism and Reinlie v. U.S., 2001 U.S. App., 239 F.3d 1280, Feb. 8, 2001.
[22] Armed Forces News, [http://www.armedforcesnews.com/backissues/2001/062201.htm] June 22, 2001.
[23] Schism and Reinlie v. U.S. 2001 WL 664440 (Fed. Cir. (Fla)), June 13, 2001.
[24] Schism and Reinlie v. United States, 2002 WL 31549178 (Fed.Cir.(Fla.)), November 18, 2002.
[25] Hamby, James E., Jr., "Free care for life is a myth," Air Force Times, September 20, 1993: 18.
[26] See, for example, Rich, Spencer, Military Health Care Downsizing Leaves Retirees in a Bind, Washington, Post, July 30, 1996: A11; Editorials, Veterans should not be force to pay for "free" health care, Kerrville Daily Times, December 8, 1997: 4A; "... the promise of free health care in their later years was a major enticement to stay for a full career.", AFSA Calls for Tricare Reform, Sergeants, November 1995: 9; Kaczor, Bill, AP, Miami Herald, Military Retirees Appealing Benefits Denial, December 12, 1998: "At the heart of the matter is a 1956 law that permits free care for retirees at military hospitals and clinics but only on a space[-]available basis." and, Joyce, Terry, Network Offers Health Care Answers For Military Families, Charleston Post and Courier, January 9, 2000, "Folks who are upset about care that's no longer available or cash outlays for what was supposed to be free."

Notably, certain former recruiters claim to have made such promises. They may well have. Nevertheless, as pointed out above, unauthorized promises based on mistakes, fraud, etc., do not constitute a contractual obligation on the part of the government/taxpayer.

In a different vein, others suggest that although no such **legal** entitlement exists, a **moral** obligation or an obligation based on popular opinion is sufficiently compelling to make such a promise a reality. For example, Hon. Stephen Joseph, former Assistant Secretary of Defense (Health Affairs) stated before a congressional subcommittee in 1995:

> The lawyers will tell you that there is no fine print that says free medical care guaranteed for life. I think though it is facetious for anybody to sit up here and say that, that is not what recruits believe when they are talked to by their recruiter. That is a fact of life.[27]

Whether there is or should be a moral obligation is a matter of opinion; as decided by the courts and enforced by the administrators, these claims, like the others, do not create a contractual obligation on the part of the government/taxpayer. The courts, and other analysts, have noted that allowing these claims to create such an obligation would thwart the constitutional role of Congress (i.e., prevent the Congress from determining the compensation and benefits of the armed forces) and create a situation wherein military personnel/retirees (and potentially all other federal employees) could create or expand their own benefits with popular myth or rumor and without review.

Despite extensive documentation, including court decisions, to the contrary, the belief in legally guaranteed "free lifetime care" persists,[28] and such claims continue color debate over the availability of these and other military health care benefits.[29]

---

[27] U.S. Congress. House. National Security Committee, Military Personnel Subcommittee, Hearings, Oversight of Previously Authorized Programs, 104th Cong., 1st Sess., H.Rept 104-7, March 28, 1995: 828. The Retired Officer Association also credits Dr. Joseph with testifying (in 1995) "before Congress that DoD has an "implied moral commitment" to provide health care to all eligible beneficiaries."

[28] See U.S. Congress. House. National Security Committee, Military Personnel Subcommittee, Hearings on National Defense Authorization Act for Fiscal Year 1998-H.R. 1119 and Oversight of Previously Authorized Programs. HNSC No. 105-6, 105th Cong., 1st Sess., Feb. 27, 1997: 1-162, for a lengthy treatment of this issue.

[29] For example, an insert in The Retired Officer Magazine, January 1998, seeking FEHBP benefits for military retirees over 65, is entitled, "FEHBP-65: The fix for broken health care promise."

## RECENT LEGISLATION

Though Congress has never authorized "free health care for life at military facilities," various congressional reports have commented on the issue, and there have been recent legislative actions on the subject. For example, the Senate, explaining its support of additional benefits for military retirees, included non-binding language in its report on the fiscal year 1998 National Defense Authorization Act that reiterated its intention with regard to the promise of lifetime care:

> A longstanding priority of the committee has been the improvement of the military health care system ....
>
> [T]he committee is concerned that the Department of Defense (DOD) faces significant constraints on its ability to meet the entire range of benefits expected by participants in the Military Health Service System ....
>
> The issue of health care for military retirees over age 65 is of special concern to the committee. The nation has incurred a moral obligation to attempt to provide care to military retirees who believe they were promised lifetime health care in exchange for a lifetime of military service. The nation fulfills its obligation through Medicare.[30]

Here, the Senate is clearly expressing its view that a "promise" to military retirees was made - and that existing statutes and institutions do fulfill that promise.

Later, with the enactment of the FY1998 National Defense Authorization Act, Congress included the following language:

## Sec. 752. Sense of Congress Regarding Quality Health Care for Retirees

### *(A) Findings*

Congress makes the follow findings:

1) Many retired military personnel believe that they were promised lifetime heath care in exchange for 20 or more years of service.

---

[30] U.S. Congress. Senate. Committee on Armed Services, National Defense Authorization Act for Fiscal Year 1998, 105th Cong., 1st Sess., S.Rept. 105-29, S. 924, June 17, 1997: 294-5.

2) Military retirees are the only Federal Government personnel who have been prevented from using their employer-provided health care at or after 65 years of age.

3) Military health care has become increasingly difficult to obtain for military retirees as the Department of Defense reduces its health care infrastructure.

4) Military retirees deserve to have a health care program that is at least comparable with that of retirees from civilian employment by the Federal Government.

5) The availability of quality, lifetime health care is a critical recruiting incentive for the Armed Forces.

6) Quality health care is a critical aspect of the quality of life of the men and women serving in the Armed Forces.

## *(B) Sense of the Congress*

It is the sense of the Congress that:

1) The United States has incurred a moral obligation to provide health care to members and former members of the Armed Forces who are entitled to retired or retainer pay (or its equivalent);

2) It is, therefore, necessary to provide quality, affordable health care to such retirees; and,

3) Congress and the President should take steps to address the problems associated with the availability of health care for such retirees within two years after the date of the enactment of this Act.[31]

Although this language is also non-binding, it does give a sense of the rationale behind creating additional benefits for retirees.[32]

---

[31] P.L. 105-85, sec. 752, November 18, 1997.
[32] These additional benefits include the creation of demonstration projects known as Medicare Subvention and a Federal Employees Health Benefits Program option. In addition, Congress has instructed DOD to insure an improved pharmaceutical benefit for eligible beneficiaries. For additional information, see CRS Issue Brief IB93103, Military Medical Care: Questions and Answers, by Richard Best, updated regularly.

Some in Congress would like to go further in clarifying the issue. On August 6, 1998, Rep. Jo Ann Emerson (R., MO), introduced legislation that would have established a "Medicare eligible military retiree health care consensus task force."

Among its proposed duties, this task force would conduct "a comprehensive legal and factual study of ... [p]romises, commitments, or representations made to members of the Uniformed Service by Department of Defense personnel with respect to health care coverage of such members and their families after separation from the Uniformed Services."[33] The twelve-member task force (including representatives of military retiree organizations) would determine what had been promised to military members and to what extent these promises were binding. This legislation was reintroduced in the 107th Congress.[34]

One reported response to this legislation by an unidentified representative of a military retiree organization was somewhat muted, suggesting that "... we are really beyond the point of looking at broken promises. We are at the stage now where Congress knows something has to be done and is just trying to decide what to do."[35] The legislation was referred to committee but was not reported out of committee prior to adjournment.

As noted above, H.R. 2966 was introduced on September 28, 1999. (This legislation was followed by H.R. 3573, S. 2003 and S. 2013 which have very similar, albeit not identical, provisions.) Among their provisions, H.R. 2966, H.R. 3573, S. 2003, and S. 2013 seek to expand military retiree health care options to include access to the Federal Employees Health Benefits Program. In offering these benefits, these bills present a number of "findings" (some of which appear inconsistent with the official history of military medical care). For example, H.R. 2966, H.R. 3573 and S. 2003 find that:

> Statutes enacted in 1956 entitled those who entered service on or after June 7, 1956, and retired after serving a minimum of 20 years or by reason of a service-connected disability, to medical and dental care in any facility of the uniformed services, subject to the availability of space and facilities and the capabilities of the medical and dental staff.

In addition to not being consistent with the statute, the Department of Defense has always maintained that military retiree health care is, and always has been, permissive in nature and therefore not an entitlement. (See page 5, above.)

---

[33] H.R. 4464, August 6, 1998: 2.
[34] H.R. 67, January 3, 2001.
[35] Cited as "a representative of a major military organization" lobbying for improved medical care for military retirees; see Maze, Rick, A Broken Promise, Navy Times, August 24, 1998: 24.

As noted above, although none of these bills was enacted, Congress substantially expanded the health care benefits available to military retirees via the FY2001 National Defense Authorization Act. Among its provisions, this legislation provides an enhanced pharmacy benefit and, with certain restrictions, it extends Tricare coverage to those age 65 and older (known as "Tricare for Life").

*Chapter 3*

# MILITARY MEDICAL CARE SERVICES

## *Richard A. Best, Jr.*

### INTRODUCTION

The primary mission of the Military Health Services System (MHSS), which encompasses the Defense Department's hospitals, clinics, and medical personnel, is to maintain the health of military personnel so they can carry out their military missions, and to be prepared to deliver health care during wartime. The military medical system also provides, where space is available, health care services in Department of Defense (DOD) medical facilities to dependents of active duty service members and to retirees and their dependents.

The Civilian Health and Medical Program of the Uniformed Services (CHAMPUS) was established in 1966 as the military equivalent of a health insurance plan, run by DOD, for active duty dependents, military retirees, and the dependents of retirees, survivors of deceased members, and certain former spouses. CHAMPUS reimburses beneficiaries for portions of the costs of health care received from civilian providers.

As a follow-on to CHAMPUS, DOD has established Tricare to coordinate the efforts of the services' medical facilities. Tricare will also provide beneficiaries with the opportunity to receive their care through a DOD-managed health maintenance organization, a preferred provider organization, or to continue to use regular CHAMPUS (now known as Tricare Standard).

The MHSS currently includes some 76 hospitals and 513 clinics serving an eligible population of 8.2 million. It operates worldwide and employs some 38,000 civilians and 92,000 active duty military personnel. For FY2001, appropriations for military medicine totaled some $19.1 billion (including $5.3 in military personnel costs. Appropriations for FY2002 reached $24.2 billion as a result of expanded benefits authorized in 2000 that took effect in 2001.

Although CHAMPUS was intended to provide retirees with health care benefits from the time of their retirement, usually in their mid-40s, the FY2001 Defense Authorization Act provided that Tricare serve as a second payer to Medicare for retirees and their spouses and survivors beginning in FY2002. The Act also extended a pharmacy benefit to Medicare-eligible beneficiaries. This program is known as Tricare for Life (TFL).

Some retirees groups advocate opening the Federal Employees Health Benefits Program (FEHBP) to military retirees, but an FEHBP demonstration project did not prove very popular among beneficiaries.

## Most Recent Developments

On March 10, 2003, the Defense Department extended medical benefits for activated reserve component personnel and their dependents. First, reservists now become eligible for medical benefits if called to active duty for more than 30 days and their dependents residing in Tricare Prime catchment areas can enroll in Tricare Prime. Previously, such benefits were only available for reservists called for more than 179 days of active duty. Dependents not residing in areas where Tricare Prime is available are now eligible for Tricare Prime Remote and can receive the same level of medical treatment at costs comparable to those incurred by active duty personnel.

## Background and Analysis

Although the Military Health Services System (MHSS) is primarily designed to provide medical services to active duty service members, it is also a major source of medical care, in both military and civilian facilities, to the dependents of active duty personnel, military retirees, and retirees' dependents. Since 1967 civilian care to millions of dependents and retirees (and retirees' dependents) has been provided through the Civilian Health and Medical Program of the Uniformed Services (CHAMPUS) although beneficiaries are responsible for certain co-payments. Since 1995 the Department of Defense (DOD) has sought to coordinate the medical care efforts of the Army, Navy, and Air Force, and to institute managed care principles in a program known as Tricare. Tricare provides beneficiaries with the opportunity of choosing a health maintenance organization option, a preferred provider option, or a fee-for-service option.

The implementation of Tricare and other efforts to manage DOD health care more efficiently as well as downsize the MHSS as part of the overall post-cold war reductions of the entire Defense Department, meant that less care was available to non-active duty beneficiaries, especially to those aged 65 and over. Informed, articulate, and well-organized, this population sought authorization to obtain health care benefits after they became eligible for Medicare. The Defense Authorization Act for FY2001 (P.L. 106-259) provided for both a pharmacy benefit and access to Tricare for those who became Medicare-eligible at age 65.

This issue brief attempts to answer basic questions about the MHSS, its beneficiary population, the medical services it provides, its costs, and major changes that are underway or have been proposed. Citations are made to more detailed CRS studies where appropriate. The General Accounting Office (GAO) and the Congressional Budget Office (CBO) have also published important studies. In addition, the Office of the Assistant Secretary of Defense for Health Affairs Home Page may be of interest [http://www.tricare.osd.mil/].

## QUESTIONS AND ANSWERS

### 1. What Is the Purpose of the Military Health Services System?

The MHSS provides medical care to active duty military personnel, eligible military retirees, and eligible dependents of both groups. The primary mission of the medical services system is to maintain the health of military personnel, so they can carry out their military missions, and to be prepared to deliver health care required during wartime. Often described as the medical readiness mission, this effort involves medical testing and screening of recruits, emergency medical treatment of servicemen and women involved in hostilities, and the maintenance of physical standards of those in the armed services.

In support of those in uniform, the military medical system also provides, where space is available, health care services to dependents of active duty service members. Space available care is also provided to retirees and their dependents. Some former spouses are also included. Since 1966 civilian medical care for dependents of active duty personnel, and for retirees and their dependents who are under age 65 has been available (with certain limitations and co-payments) through the Civilian Health and Medical Program of the Uniformed Services (CHAMPUS). Since October 2001 Tricare benefits have been available to retirees and their dependents aged 65 and over.

## 2. What is the Structure of the Military Health Services System?

Under the Secretary of Defense, the MHSS is headed by the Assistant Secretary of Defense for Health Affairs (ASD/HA). An October 1991 reorganization strengthened the role of the ASD/HA by giving the incumbent planning, programming, and budgeting responsibilities for the MHSS, including facilities operated by the Army, Navy (which also provides health care services to the Marine Corps), and Air Force. The Surgeons General of the Army, Navy and Air Force retain considerable responsibility for managing military medical facilities and personnel.

The MHSS currently includes 76 hospitals, and 513 clinics operating worldwide and employs more than 37,000 civilians and 91,000 active duty military personnel. Direct care costs include the provision of medical care directly to beneficiaries, the administrative requirements of a large medical establishment, and maintaining a capability to provide medical care to combat forces in case of hostilities. Civilian providers under contract to the Department of Defense (DOD) have constituted a major portion of the MHSS in recent years.

Although the number of active duty personnel in DOD is not projected to increase over the next few years, costs associated with the MHSS are not expected to follow suit. This results from general inflation in the cost of health care and an increasing percentage of care being provided to retirees and their dependents. (In 1950 retirees made up 8% of those eligible for military health care; by 1997 it was over 50%.) Reductions in direct care can actually lead to growth in overall DOD health spending because beneficiaries whose access to military medical facilities is removed through base closures may turn to more costly care from civilian providers, for which they can seek reimbursement from DOD.

Each year the Office of the Secretary of Defense (OSD) forwards a budget request to Congress for the Defense Health Program (DHP), which includes monies needed for procuring equipment for the MHSS, operation and maintenance, and care for civilian beneficiaries. Funding for the compensation of military personnel assigned to the MHSS is contained in the Military Personnel appropriation accounts of the individual military departments. Additional requests are made in procurement and military construction accounts. For FY2003 the Bush Administration requested an overall figure of $26 billion including $6.1 billion for military personnel costs.

## 3. How Much Does Military Health Care Cost Beneficiaries?

Active duty service members receive covered medical care in military facilities without additional costs, other than small per diem charges. Other beneficiaries pay differing amounts depending on their status and where they receive care. If care can be obtained at military facilities, there is no charge for medical services, and only small daily charges for hospital stays.

Tricare costs vary by the option selected. Active duty personnel are automatically enrolled in Tricare Prime without any premiums; their dependents may join, also without premiums. Retirees (under age 65) must pay $230 (individual) or $460 (family) each year in enrollment fees. There have been small fees required for visits to civilian care providers who are part of the Tricare network, but DOD proposes that they be eliminated.

Tricare Standard or CHAMPUS has a more complicated cost structure. There are no premiums or enrollment fees. At present, for outpatient care in civilian hospitals and clinics, there is a yearly deductible of $150.00 for one person and $300.00 for a family (with lower fees for the most junior enlisted personnel). After the yearly deductible is met, dependents of active duty personnel pay 20% of CHAMPUS-approved care; all others pay 25%. For inpatient care, there is no deductible for CHAMPUS-approved care, but families of active duty service members pay a small per diem. Other CHAMPUS beneficiaries will pay the lesser of 25% of the billed charges or a fixed daily amount ($417. in FY2003) of care covered by CHAMPUS. In addition, there is a "cap" on annual care; active duty families are reimbursed for allowable expenses over $1000 and other CHAMPUS families are reimbursed for allowable expenses over $3,000. These figures are generalized; there are a number of important exceptions that are explained in the CHAMPUS Handbook and in the underlying Federal Regulations (32 CFR 199). The Handbook urges beneficiaries to check with their Health Benefits Advisors before seeking care.

Tricare Extra, the preferred provider option, has a cost structure similar to CHAMPUS except that beneficiaries who use health care providers in the Extra network pay 5% less than they would if using non-network providers. Inpatient care costs $12.72 per day for active duty dependents and $417. per day (or 25% of daily hospital costs, whichever is less) for retirees and their dependents. Care may still be obtained from military facilities if space is available.

## 4. In What Ways Has the MHSS Been Changing in Recent Years?

During the Cold War, the MHSS was designed to support a full-scale, extremely violent war with the Soviet Union and its allies in Europe. High casualties were anticipated along with a need for in-theater medical treatment facilities. The collapse of the Soviet Union and the end of the Warsaw Pact led to a major reassessment of U.S. defense policy. In the future, defense planners believe, the most likely conflicts will be of limited duration and involve smaller numbers of troops. The overall size of the active duty force has been reduced by one-third since the mid-1980s. Planners expect that casualties can be treated locally (with greater reliance on telemedicine) or, if necessary, evacuated to military medical facilities in the continental United States (CONUS). This strategic planning, along with associated military personnel reductions, requires a smaller MHSS, fewer military medical personnel, and the closure of a number of hospitals and clinics. In recent years, the number of military medical personnel has declined by 15% and the number of military hospital has been reduced by one-third.

On the other hand, the number of potential beneficiaries of military medical care who are over age 65 has grown in absolute terms to 1.2 million, and now represents about one-half of the beneficiary population. This number is expected to grow until 2009. Most retirees become eligible for Medicare when they reach age 65 although some disabled retirees become eligible for Medicare earlier. In 1991 Congress acted (in P.L. 102-190) to reestablish CHAMPUS eligibility for persons under age 65 who become eligible for Medicare, Part A because of disability. Such persons are, however, required to enroll in Medicare Part B (and pay premiums) to be eligible for CHAMPUS/Tricare.

In addition to revisions in military planning, nation-wide changes in the practice of medicine have also affected the MHSS. In particular, managed care initiatives and capitated budgeting that are widely adopted in the civilian community are being implemented in DOD's Tricare program. Tricare is also designed to coordinate medical care efforts of the three military departments in some 12 geographical regions, each under a single military commander known as a lead agent. The lead agents are responsible for managing care provided by all military medical facilities in their respective regions, and for contracting for additional care from civilian providers. These competitively-bid, region-wide contracts represent a significant change in delivery of defense health care and will, it is anticipated, result in cost savings. Each region will have a capitated budget based on the total number of beneficiaries in the region. Detailed regulations governing Tricare were made effective on November 1, 1995 (32 CFR 199). Although care continues to be centered around military medical facilities, heavy reliance will be placed on civilian contractors managed by the lead agent where necessary.

The centerpiece of Tricare is the Tricare Prime option, a DOD version of a health maintenance organization (HMO) that the beneficiary joins, and which provides essentially all of his or her medical care. Care is provided through DOD medical personnel, hospitals, and clinics, as well as affiliated civilian physicians, hospitals, and other providers. Costs are contained through administrative controls and treatment protocols. In civilian practice, HMOs have been credited with some success in reducing costs, although opponents of these systems complain about restrictions on provider choice and incentives that may be created to constrain the delivery of services.

CHAMPUS/Tricare Standard has been the military equivalent of a health insurance plan, run by DOD, for active duty dependents, military retirees, and the dependents of retirees, survivors of deceased members, and certain former spouses. Unlike private insurance plans, CHAMPUS/Tricare Standard does not require premiums. If care at a military facility cannot be provided (due to space limitations, limitations on the types of services that a facility is capable of providing, or due to the fact that a beneficiary may not live close enough to a military facility to make such travel reasonable), CHAMPUS/Tricare Standard will share responsibility with the beneficiary for the payment of care received from non-military health care providers, subject to regulations. If beneficiaries need inpatient care or certain types of outpatient care and live within a catchment area, i.e., a geographical area surrounding a military hospital, they must seek care first at that military medical facility and receive a document (known as a non-availability statement (NAS)) stating that the needed care was not available at that military facility, before CHAMPUS/Tricare Standard will pay a share of their care at a non-military facility. Certain types of care, such as most dentistry and chiropractic services, are excluded.

In addition to CHAMPUS/Tricare Standard and Tricare Prime there is a preferred-provider option, Tricare Extra. In Tricare Extra beneficiaries do not enroll or pay annual premiums but use physicians and specialists in the Tricare network and are charged 5% less for medical services.

Many of the changes made in the past decade have been intended to improve medical care available to the active duty population, but they have also resulted in less medical care available in military facilities for retired personnel and their dependents. The introduction of Tricare for Life in FY2002 provided coverage for retired beneficiaries, but most of their care will undoubtedly be obtained from civilian providers reimbursed by Medicare and Tricare.

## 5. Who Is Eligible to Receive This Care?

Current law provides that active duty personnel are entitled to receive health care at military medical facilities. In addition, active duty dependents, military retirees and their dependents, and survivors of deceased members are eligible to receive health care at military medical facilities when space and professional services are available. Also eligible to receive care for a fixed fee in these facilities are certain government officials (including the President and Members of Congress) and certain foreign military personnel on active duty in the U.S. Reserve Component personnel and their dependents are also entitled to care in military medical facilities under certain conditions that were extended in March 2003 to accommodate reservists called up for more than 30 days.

Since 1967 DOD has funded, under the Civilian Health and Medical Program of the Uniformed Services (CHAMPUS), care by civilian providers to dependents, retirees, and dependents of retirees who are under age 65 and unable to obtain access in a military health facility. After 1991 DOD began, with congressional support, moving towards managed care arrangements under the Tricare program that include greater use of civilian health care providers even for active duty personnel. CHAMPUS will continue but will be known as the Tricare Standard option.

## 6. How Are Priorities for Care in Military Medical Facilities Assigned?

Active duty personnel, military retirees, and their respective dependents are not afforded equal access to care in military medical facilities. Active duty personnel are entitled to health care in a military medical facility (10 USC 1074).

According to 10 U.S.C. 1076, dependents of active duty personnel are "entitled, upon request, to medical and dental care" on a space-available basis at a military medical facility. Title 10 U.S.C. 1074 states that "a member or former member of the uniformed services who is entitled to retired or retainer pay ... may, upon request, be given medical and dental care in any facility of the uniformed service" on a space-available basis.

This language entitles active duty dependents to medical and dental care subject to space-available limitations. No such entitlement or "right" is provided to retirees or their dependents. Instead, retirees and their dependents may be given medical and dental care, subject to the same space-available limitations. This language gives active duty personnel and their dependents priority in receiving medical and dental care at any facility of the uniformed services over military members entitled to receive retired pay and their dependents. The policy of providing active duty dependents priority over retirees in the receipt of medical and dental care in any facility of the uniformed services has existed in law since at least September 2, 1958 (P.L. 85-861).

Since the establishment of Tricare and pursuant to the Defense Authorization Act of FY1996 (P.L. 104-106), DOD has established the following basic priorities (with certain special provisions):

Priority 1: Active-duty service members;

Priority 2: Active-duty family members who are enrolled in Tricare Prime;

Priority 3: Retirees, their family members and survivors who are enrolled in Tricare Prime;

Priority 4: Active-duty family members who are not enrolled in Tricare Prime;

Priority 5: All other eligible persons.

The priority is given to active duty dependents to help them obtain care easily, and thus make it possible for active duty members to perform their military service without worrying about health care for their dependents. This is particularly important for active duty personnel who may be assigned overseas or aboard ship and separated from their dependents. As retirees are not subject to such imposed separations, they are considered to be in a better position to see that their dependents receive care, if care cannot be provided in a military facility. Thus, the role of health care delivery recognizes the unique needs of the military mission. The role of health care in the military is qualitatively different, and, therefore, not necessarily comparable to the civilian sector.

The benefits (including Tricare/CHAMPUS) available to service members or retirees, which require comparatively little or no contributions from the beneficiaries themselves, are considered by some to be a more generous benefit package than is available to civil servants or to most people in the private sector. Retirees may also be eligible to receive medical care at Department of Veterans' Affairs (VA) medical facilities.

## 7. What is the Relationship of DOD Health Care to Medicare?

Active duty military personnel have been fully covered by Social Security and have paid Social Security taxes since Jan. 1, 1957. Social Security coverage includes eligibility for health care coverage under Medicare at age 65. It was the legislative intent of the Congress that retired members of the uniformed services and their eligible dependents be provided with medical care after they retire from the military, usually between their late-30s and mid-40s. CHAMPUS was intended to supplement - not to replace - military health care. Likewise, Congress did not intend that CHAMPUS should replace Medicare as a supplemental benefit to military health care. For this reason, retirees become ineligible to receive CHAMPUS benefits when at age 65 they become eligible for Medicare. Many argue that the structure is inherently unfair because retirees lose Tricare/CHAMPUS benefits at the stage in life when they are increasingly likely to need them. Military retirees continue to be eligible for health care in military medical care facilities irrespective of age if space is available. The FY2001 Defense Authorization Act (P.L. 106-259) provided that, beginning October 1, 2001, Tricare will pay out-of-pocket costs for services provided under Medicare for beneficiaries over age 64 if they are enrolled in Medicare Part B. Disabled persons under 65 who are entitled to Medicare may continue to receive CHAMPUS benefits as a second payer to Medicare Parts A and B (with some restrictions). For additional information regarding eligibility of Medicare eligible persons under age 65, see above, Question 4.

## 8. Have Military Personnel Been Promised Free Medical Care for Life?

Some military personnel and former military personnel maintain that they and their dependents were promised "free medical care for life" at the time of their enlistment. Such promises may have been made by military recruiters and in recruiting brochures; however, if they were made, they were not based upon laws or official regulations which provide only for access to military medical facilities for non-active duty personnel if space is available as described above. Space was not always available and Tricare options could involve significant costs to beneficiaries. Rear Admiral Harold M. Koenig, the Deputy Assistant Secretary of Defense for Health Affairs, testified in May 1993: "We have a medical care program for life for our beneficiaries, and it is pretty well defined in the law. That easily gets interpreted to, or reinterpreted into, free medical care for the rest of your life. That is a pretty easy transition for people to make in their thinking, and it is pervasive. We [DOD] spend an incredible amount of effort trying to re-educate people [that] that is not their benefit." (U.S. Congress, House of Representatives, Committee on Armed Services, Military Forces and Personnel Subcommittee, 103rd Congress, 1st session, National Defense Authorization Act for Fiscal Year 1994 - H.R. 2401 and Oversight of Previously Authorized Programs, Hearings, H.A.S.C. No. 103-13, April 27, 28, May 10, 11, and 13, 1993, p. 505.)

Dr. Stephen C. Joseph, Assistant Secretary of Defense for Health Affairs until April 1998, however, argued that because retirees believe they have had a promise of free care, the government did have an obligation. Joseph did not specify the precise extent of the obligation. The FY1998 Defense Authorization Act (P.L. 105-85) included (in Section 752) a finding that "many retired military personnel believe that they were promised lifetime health care in exchange for 20 or more years of service," and expressed the sense of Congress that "the United States has incurred a moral obligation to provide health care to members and [retired] members of the Armed Services." Further, it is necessary "to provide quality, affordable care to such retirees."

## 9. What Actions Are Being Taken to Improve Military Medical Care for Retirees Aged 65 and Over? What is Tricare for Life?

As noted above, military medical care is theoretically available to all retirees on a space- available basis. As a practical matter, however, the amount of space available to retirees over age 65 who are eligible for Medicare has become increasingly limited. This results from base closures, changing approaches to military medicine, and growth in the number of retirees. Retirees and retiree organizations have complained of being frozen out of military facilities, of being responsible for higher costs at a stage of life when more health care is required, and, especially, of the burden of having to pay for expensive pharmaceuticals that are taken on a regular basis.

As a result of legislation in the 105th and 106th Congresses, several demonstration projects were established in specific localities to assess beneficiary acceptance and the fiscal viability of different approaches. These included:

- **Medicare subvention** by which care would be provided by DOD to retirees age 65 and over essentially on the same basis as is provided to retirees under 65 in Tricare Prime [enrollment fees of $230/460 (self/self+dependent) are required annually]; the legislation provides that DOD would be reimbursed for a portion of the costs of this care by Medicare. (The Medicare subvention demonstration project was established by Section 4015 of the Budget Reconciliation Act of 1998 (P.L. 105-33); it was a 3-year project (termed Tricare Senior Prime) at six sites that was phased in beginning in July 1998 and scheduled to conclude in December 2001.)
- Access to the FEHBP plans used by civil service retirees with DOD paying the same share of premiums that is paid by the government for civilian enrollees (approximately 72%). (An FEHBP demonstration was established by Section 721 of the FY1999 Defense Authorization Act (P.L. 105-261); it was conducted at eight sites for 3 years, ending December 31, 2002.)
- Tricare as a supplement to Medicare. Established by Section 722 of the FY1999 Defense Authorization Act (P.L. 105-261), this program was scheduled to begin in 2000 and end in December 2002 but was overtaken by the establishment of Tricare for Life.
- A DOD-sponsored pharmaceutical benefit. The FY2001 Defense Authorization Act (P.L. 106-398) extended pharmacy benefits to all retirees beginning in April 2001. Beneficiaries who became 65 before April 1, 2001, do not have to enroll in Medicare Part B to receive the DOD pharmacy benefit; those who turned 65 on or after April 1, 2001, have to be enrolled in Medicare Part B to use the pharmacy benefit.

On February 12, 1998, the Administration announced that the Medicare subvention demonstration, to be known as Tricare Senior Prime, would be conducted at Keesler Air Force Base, Biloxi, Miss.; Brooke Army Medical Center and Wilford Hall Medical Center, San Antonio, Texas, Fort Sill, Lawton, Okla., Sheppard Air Force Base, Wichita Falls, Texas; Fort Carson and the Air Force Academy, Colorado Springs, Co.; Madigan Army Medical Center, Fort Lewis, Wash.; Naval Medical Center, San Diego, CA.; and Dover Air Force Base, Dover,

Del. Enrollments for the Madigan demonstration began in July 1998. The demonstration project ended on December 31, 2001.

On January 14, 1999, the Defense Department announced sites for the FEHBP demonstrations. They were Dover Air Force Base, Delaware; Commonwealth of Puerto Rico; Fort Knox, Kentucky; Greensboro/Winston-Salem/High Point, North Carolina; Dallas, Texas; Humboldt County, California area; Naval Hospital, Camp Pendleton, California; and New Orleans, Louisiana. Coverage started in January 2000 and ended in December 2002. Beneficiaries had to enroll in an FEHBP plan and pay applicable premiums; the government's contribution was computed the same as it has been for other FEHBP enrollees. Those who were eligible included over-65 retirees who are eligible for Medicare and their dependents, unremarried former spouses of military members, and dependents of deceased members or former members.

The FY1999 Defense Authorization Act (P.L. 105-261) also directed a demonstration project that would have Tricare serve as a supplement to Medicare. Scheduled to begin in 2000 and last through the end of 2002, the Tricare Senior Supplement Demonstration Program is conducted in Cherokee, Texas, and Santa Clara, California. Those who live in those locations and choose to participate will have to pay an enrollment fee (as well as join Medicare Part B), but Tricare will cover some costs that are not covered by Medicare.

On August 16, 1999, DOD announced that the Tricare Pilot Pharmacy Benefit projects would be established during 2000 in Okeechobee, Florida and Fleming, Kentucky.

In late 1999 and early 2000, a number of bills were introduced to provide more extensive medical care options to beneficiaries aged 65 and over. Some of the bills would extend the durations of the demonstration projects or expand them nationwide; others would have DOD pay 100% of FEHBP premiums for certain older retirees. All such proposals would entail significant expenditures.

During consideration of the FY2001 Defense Authorization Bill (H.R. 4205) on May 18, 2000, the House adopted an amendment that would extend Medicare subvention nationwide by 2006. During consideration of its version of the FY2001 Defense Authorization Bill (S. 2549), the Senate on June 7, 2000, adopted an amendment that would extend eligibility for participation in Tricare to beneficiaries over age 64. The provision would take effect in October 2001; Medicare would serve as a first payer for services provided, with Tricare providing reimbursement for some types of care that Medicare does not cover. Beneficiaries would be required to participate in Medicare Part B. Another floor amendment that would have included retiree access not only to Tricare but also to FEHBP (with the government paying all premiums for those whose service began before June 1956) failed on a procedural vote that required support by three-fifths of the senators. In late August 2000, the Clinton Administration indicated opposition to these initiatives to extend Tricare to beneficiaries over age 64 because of concerns with potential costs.

The Senate amendment was essentially adopted by the Conference Committee along with provisions establishing a Medicare-eligible retiree health care fund which would accumulate regular transfers of funds from DOD to pay for Tricare benefits to Medicare- eligible beneficiaries. The Conference version was adopted by large majorities in the House on October 11 and in the Senate on October 12 and was signed into law on October 30, 2000, becoming P.L. 106-398.

Beginning October 1, 2001, for beneficiaries over age 64 who are enrolled in Medicare Part B, the Defense Department, through a program known as **Tricare for Life (TFL)** is serving as a second payer to Medicare, paying out-of-pocket costs for medical services covered under Medicare. The beneficiaries are also eligible for medical benefits covered by Tricare but not by Medicare.

The requirement for enrollment in Medicare Part B, which currently costs $54.00 per month, is a source of concern to some beneficiaries, especially those who did not enroll in Part B when they became 65 and thus must pay significant penalties. Some argue that this requirement is unfair since Part B enrollment was not until this year a prerequisite for access to any DOD medical care. On the other hand, waiving the penalty for military retirees could be considered unfair to other Medicare-users who did not enroll in Part B upon turning 65.

## 10. What is Medicare Subvention? Should Medicare Reimburse DOD for Care Provided to Medicare-eligible Beneficiaries?

Current law generally prohibits Medicare from paying for services provided or paid for by another governmental entity (Section 1862(a)(3) of the Social Security Act (42 USC 1395y)). Medicare subvention is the term given to proposals that Medicare (specifically, the Health Care Financing Administration (HCFA) [more recently the Centers for Medicare and Medicaid Services (CMS)] of the Department of Health and Human Services) reimburse DOD for care provided to Medicare-eligible beneficiaries at DOD facilities or through Tricare. (It is estimated that currently some $1.2 billion annually is spent by DOD to provide care for Medicare-eligible beneficiaries.) In other words, when care is given by DOD to a retiree or dependent who is over age 65, Medicare would be asked to reimburse DOD according to an agreed-upon rate, much as Medicare would reimburse a civilian physician who provides care to an eligible person.

Advocates of Medicare subvention claimed that military retirees, even those over age 65, were promised "free health care for the rest of their lives" by military recruiters and have come to expect it, regardless of "legal technicalities." They argued that ending access to military medical facilities when beneficiaries reach an age when they will have greater need for it is fundamentally unfair. Reimbursement from Medicare would provide an important revenue source that will enable and encourage DOD to provide care to over-65 retirees. Further, it was argued that Medicare will save money because DOD can provide care less expensively than civilian providers (largely because of more austere facilities).

Opponents of Medicare subvention pointed out that there has never been a statutory guarantee that retirees and their dependents would have "free health care to the rest of their lives." In accordance with congressional intent, CHAMPUS has served as a health insurance system to cover military personnel until they became eligible for Medicare at age 65. Retirees over age 65, they note, continue to have access to military medical facilities on a space-available basis. A major concern was the widely perceived need to curtail rather than expand Medicare spending. Additional spending under a subvention proposal, if it was to be required, would necessitate further Medicare spending reductions. Some observers expressed concern that subvention could, in particular, lead to greater costs to Medicare if DOD care attracts beneficiaries who are currently using non-government health care plans. The transfer of funds from Medicare, an entitlement program, to the discretionary accounts of DOD, and thus subject to the annual authorization/appropriation process, would be complicated, given the provisions for budget enforcement. Further, some observers believe that giving DOD greater responsibilities for geriatric medicine may compete with its combat readiness mission.

In the 104th Congress, several Medicare subvention bills were introduced. Language in the FY1996 Defense Authorization Act expressed the sense of Congress that DOD should be reimbursed by Medicare for care given by DOD to Medicare-eligible beneficiaries in areas where Tricare is implemented. On June 20, 1996 the Senate approved an amendment to the FY1997 Defense Authorization Bill (S. 1745) that required the Administration to submit by September 6, 1996 "a specific plan" for a demonstration project that would permit Medicare-eligible beneficiaries to enroll in the managed care Tricare option. Medicare would reimburse DOD on a capitated basis for beneficiaries who choose to enroll. The requirement for a plan for a demonstration project was included in the subsequent conference version (H.R. 3230) and a draft plan was circulated by the Administration, but no mandate for implementing a plan was enacted in the 104th Congress and the legislation as signed (P.L. 104-201) did not authorize spending for a Medicare subvention demonstration project nor were funds appropriated for this purpose.

In the 105th Congress, Section 4015 of the Budget Reconciliation Act (P.L. 105-33), signed into law on August 5, 1997, included complex provisions authorizing the establishment of a three-year Medicare subvention demonstration project at six sites. DOD would be reimbursed by Medicare at a rate equal to 95% of that paid to Medicare+Choice HMOs. The aggregate amounts to be reimbursed under this section will not exceed $50 million for FY1998, $60 million for FY1999, and $65 million for FY2000. The Act stipulates that "no new military treatment facilities will be built or expanded with funds from the demonstration project." Medicare HMOs are authorized to enter into contracts in which DOD will provide care to Medicare-eligible military retirees and their dependents and receive reimbursement from the HMOs. A separate component of the effort will allow retirees enrolled in a limited number of Medicare+Choice plans to contract with DOD military facilities to provide specialty and inpatient care to military retirees in those plans. The FY2001 Defense Authorization Act (P.L. 106-398) extended the Medicare subvention demonstration to the end of 2001.

Although necessary data is not yet available, some observers express concern that the formula used to reimburse DOD for care provided to Medicare-eligible beneficiaries may not result in transfers of significant funds from Medicare to DOD. Tricare for Life as initiated in 2001 incorporates some aspects of Medicare subvention, but it does involve transfers of funds from Medicare to DOD.

## 11. Should the Federal Employees Health Benefits Program (FEHBP) Be Open to Military Retirees?

Some have advocated making the health care plans for Federal civil servants and civil service retirees also available to Medicare-eligible military retirees instead of or in addition to Medicare subvention plans. The civil service system, known as the Federal Employees Health Benefits Program (FEHBP), is widely considered to be successful. It allows beneficiaries to choose among a number of health care plans. The government pays some 72% of the premiums and beneficiaries are responsible for the rest. Opening FEHBP to Medicare-eligible military retirees would cause minor administrative expenses, but subsidizing annual enrollment fees for retirees and their dependents over 65 could involve around $2 billion annually (if the government paid 72% of average premiums), according to a Congressional Budget Office estimate. On the other hand, an FEHBP option would allow retirees to choose the type of health care plan they prefer and it would not affect the delivery of military medical care to the active duty population. In addition, FEHBP plans would also ensure the availability of care in geographic areas that might not be reached by Tricare options. Some potential beneficiaries, however, would not be willing to make the substantial premiums that are required for participation in FEHBP.

Despite objections from the Defense Department, the FY1999 Defense Authorization Act (P.L. 105-261) included a FEHBP demonstration project limited to 66,000 participants in 6-10 geographic areas. (Beneficiaries would not be required to participate in Medicare Part B (which requires a monthly premium) but will be urged to do so.) At least one area will be near a Military Treatment Facility (MTF); one will not. One area will be an area in which a Medicare Subvention demonstration has been underway. There will be no more than one area for each Tricare region. Enrollees will have to pay the same level of premiums as paid by civil servants and agree not to seek care in MTFs during the length of the demonstration. The Defense Department will contribute the rest of the premiums. The demonstration project began in January 2000 and ran for three years; it will be evaluated by the Defense Department and the GAO. By late 1999 it was evident that relatively few retirees would opt for FEHBP coverage (only 2000 persons had enrolled by March 2000, out of 70,000 eligible); the initial open season was extended and additional brochures were mailed out.

Legislation introduced in the 106th Congress and in the 107th (H.R. 179) would have extended FEHBP eligibility to military retirees. Some bills include provisions by which DOD would pay the entire costs of FEHBP for those retirees (and their families) who served prior to June 7, 1956 (since statutory medical benefits for retiree medical care came into force on that date). Such a proposal has been estimated to cost over $4 billion annually.

The FEHBP demonstration was completed at the end of 2002, but enrollees are eligible for other Tricare options.

## 12. How are User's Fees and Fee Schedules for Medical Services Assessed?

User's fees for medical services represent a means of generating revenues from those who use the services. In recent years user's fees, also known as co-payments, have been considered as a means of generating revenues in the military medical care system. Some observers see increased users' fees as a primary way to increase beneficiaries' cost-consciousness, arguing that far more than premiums and deductibles, cost-sharing discourages unnecessary medical services. The consideration of these fees has been subject to strong opposition from military personnel, retirees, and others who have viewed free or inexpensive health care as an important benefit of military service. To these individuals, user's fees represent an "erosion of earned benefits." Specifically, these benefits are not viewed by some beneficiaries as an insurance program paid for in a market context, but rather as a benefit that is earned by the unique nature of demands inherent in performing military service.

By law (P.L. 102-396), health care providers treating Tricare/CHAMPUS patients cannot bill for more than 115% of charges authorized by a DOD fee schedule. In some geographic areas, providers have been unwilling to accept Tricare/CHAMPUS patients because of the limits on fees that can be charged. DOD has authority to grant exceptions. Efforts have been made to bring payment levels for health care services provided by the MHSS into alignment with the Medicare's fee schedule. Over 90% of Tricare payment levels are now equivalent to those authorized by Medicare, about 10% are higher, and steps are being taken to raise some to Medicare levels.

## 13. What Will Be the Effect of Base Relocations and Closures on Military Medical Care?

Base relocations and closures undertaken as part of the restructuring of the Defense Department in the post-Cold War period have included changes in the military health services system. As a result of Base Realignment and Closure (BRAC) actions, 35% of the DOD medical treatment facilities providing services in 1987 were closed by the end of 1997 (although the number of eligible beneficiaries decreased by only 9%). Criteria for realignments and closures, established by DOD with congressional consent, include the need to deploy a force structure capable of protecting the national security, anticipated funding levels, and a number of military, fiscal, and environmental considerations that encompass community economic impact and community infrastructure.

Three Base Realignment and Closure Commissions have specifically considered the effect of closing DOD hospitals and clinics on active duty military personnel as well as on other beneficiaries and potential beneficiaries of the MHSS. The first two BRAC Commissions recommended 18 military hospital closures; the third BRAC Commission recommended an additional 10. Facilities closed include hospitals in Philadelphia, PA; Oakland, CA; Orlando, FL; San Francisco, CA; Ft. Devens, MA; Ft. Ord, CA; and Long Beach, CA. In one case, the commission overruled a DOD proposal to close the Naval Hospital in Charleston, SC.

With congressional encouragement, DOD has developed transition medical plans for certain closure sites. Medicare-eligible users of closed military hospitals will be encouraged to avail themselves of HMO and pharmacy programs established by the Department of Health and Human Services or a mail-order pharmacy system being established by DOD. Nonetheless, the closure of military hospitals and clinics can be a source of anxiety, especially in communities that have attracted large numbers of new residents seeking access to the MHSS.

## 14. What is the DOD Pharmacy Benefit?

According to DOD officials, the pharmacy benefit is the one most in demand by beneficiaries. GAO has estimated that it costs some $1.3 billion annually. Those with access to military treatment facilities and those who are enrolled in Tricare Prime receive prescribed pharmaceuticals free of charge. Users of Tricare Extra and Tricare Standard are reimbursed for pharmaceuticals in accordance with the same schedule of deductibles and co-payments required for other medical services. In accordance with the provisions of the FY2001 Defense Authorization Act (P.L. 106-398), effective April 1, 2001, retirees over age have access to DOD's National Mail Order Pharmacy and retail pharmacies in addition to pharmacies in military treatment facilities. Beneficiaries who turned 65 prior to April 1, 2001 qualify for the benefit whether or not they purchased Medicare Part B; beneficiaries who attain the age of 65 on or after April 1, 2001 must be enrolled in Medicare Part B to receive the pharmacy benefit. (There will be deductibles for use of non-network pharmacies and co-payments for pharmaceuticals received from the National Mail Order Pharmacy and from retail pharmacies.) In its first year, the pharmacy benefit saw the processing of 10.2 million prescriptions and accounted for over $562 million in drug costs.

Military pharmacies do not necessarily carry every pharmaceutical available; thus, even some with access to military facilities must have certain prescriptions filled in civilian pharmacies; for these prescriptions beneficiaries can be reimbursed through Tricare/CHAMPUS. In October 1997, DOD implemented the National Mail Order Pharmacy Program that allows beneficiaries to obtain some pharmaceuticals by mail with small handling charges. The mail order program is designed to fill long-term prescriptions to treat conditions such as high blood pressure, asthma, or diabetes; it does not include medications that require immediate attention such as some antibiotics.

The Defense Department is currently considering revisions to its pharmacy program that would encourage use of pharmaceutical included in an established formulary, i.e. an inventory of pharmaceuticals chosen for clinical effectiveness and cost effectiveness. Other pharmaceuticals would remain available but require somewhat higher co-payments by beneficiaries (generally, non-formulary prescriptions could cost beneficiaries $22 instead of the $3-$9 currently charged for 30+ day supplies).

## SELECTED LEGISLATION FROM THE 107TH CONGRESS

Military health care issues are addressed in annual Defense authorization and appropriations bills.

P.L. 107-20, H.R. 2216. Makes supplemental appropriations for FY2001, including funds for the Defense Health Program. Introduced as an original measure, June 19, 2001.

Passed House June 20; passed Senate, amended, July 10. Conference report (H.Rept. 107-148) filed July 19. Conference report passed House and Senate July 20. Signed into law July 24, 2001.

H.R. 179 (Shows). Extends coverage under the Federal Employees Health Benefits Program to military retirees. Introduced January 3, 2001; referred to the Committees on Government Reform and Armed Services.

H.R. 997 (Mink). Waives penalties for Tricare beneficiaries enrolling in Medicare Part B after age 65. Introduced March 13, 2001; referred to the Committees on Armed Services, Energy and Commerce, and Ways and Means.

H.R. 2073 (Cardin). Waives Medicare Part B late enrollment penalties for military retirees. Introduced and referred to the Committees on Energy and Commerce and Ways and Means, June 6, 2001.

*Chapter 4*

# VETERANS' PENSIONS: FACT SHEET

## *Dennis W. Snook and Alice D. Butler*

Wartime veterans and their survivors are assured of income support if disabilities render them unemployable, and if they do not have sufficient assets to provide for their own maintenance. Called *veterans' pensions* and administered by the Department of Veterans Affairs (VA), monthly cash payments are made to qualified veterans or survivors so that their total income from all countable sources reach specified annual levels. Separate support levels are established for veterans and survivors. These levels are higher for permanently housebound recipients, for those needing a paid attendant, and for those with qualified dependents. Support levels for these veterans and survivors are annually adjusted to reflect changes in the cost-of-living as measured by the Consumer Price Index (CPI). This fact sheet will be updated annually for changes in data.

In FY2000, total veterans' pension outlays were estimated to be $3.1 billion. Payments were made to an estimated 373,000 veterans and 266,000 survivors, a caseload decline from the previous year of 3% and 5%, respectively. For FY2000, it is estimated that benefits averaged $6,286 for veterans and $2,657 for survivors, annually. In 46% of the total pension caseload, the pension is based on wartime service in World War II or earlier.

## PROGRAM DESCRIPTION

The *need-tested* veterans' pension is one of several systems of cash benefits granted to veterans of military service; others being VA *compensation* (granted for disabilities incurred during military service), and Department of Defense *disability pay* (granted when a disability stops military service after the serviceperson has completed at least 8 years active duty), and *retired pay* (granted at completion of a military career). Veterans' compensation and military disability or retired pay are recompense for sacrifices and longevity attributed to a period of military service. Veterans' pensions are income guarantees earned by virtue of service during wartime and paid to totally and permanently disabled individuals who meet income eligibility.

Eligibility for a veterans' pension requires a discharge (other than dishonorable) from active service of 90 days or more, at least one of which must have been served during a period defined in law as a period of war. The veteran must be disabled for reasons neither traceable to military service nor to willful misconduct. There is no disability requirement for eligible survivors.

## BENEFITS

The VA pays monthly amounts to qualified veterans after considering other sources of income, including Social Security, retirement, annuity payments, and income of a dependent spouse or child, to bring their incomes to the above support levels. Levels are increased by $2,109 annually for veterans with service in World War I or earlier, in recognition of the absence for those veterans of education and home loan benefits available to veterans of later wars. Countable income can be reduced for unreimbursed medical expenses, as well as some educational expenses incurred by veterans or their dependents. Pensions are not payable to veterans with substantial assets. Pensions awarded before 1979 were paid under one of two programs, referred to as *Old Law* and *Prior Law*, both of which were governed by complex rules regarding countable income and exclusions. Applications beginning January 1, 1979 were processed under the *Improved Law* program, which provided higher benefits but eliminated most exclusions, offsetting countable income dollar-for-dollar. In FY2000, about 92% of veterans and 70% of survivors drew their benefits under improved law.

**Table 1.** Maximum Annual Benefits: December 2000
($ in thousands)

|  | Veteran | Survivor |
|---|---|---|
| Beneficiary without dependent | $9,304 | $6,237 |
| With one dependent | 12,186 | 8,168 |
| Permanently housebound w/o dependent | 11,372 | 7,625 |
| With one dependent | 14,253 | 9,551 |
| Needing regular aid and attendance w/o dependent | 15,524 | 9,973 |
| With one dependent | 18,405 | 11,900 |
| Each additional dependent | 1,586 | 1,586 |

**Source:** Table prepared by the Congressional Research Service (**CRS**) using data provided by the Veterans Benefits Administration.

In comparison, 1999 poverty thresholds for persons aged 65 and over were $7,990 per year for single persons and $10,869 for two persons, according to Census Bureau estimates published in the September 2000 Current Population Survey.

Veterans drawing VA pensions are automatically eligible for VA medical benefits for the treatment of nonservice-connected conditions. In FY1997 (the last year for which data are available), 72,000 pension recipients were discharged from VA medical centers (including transfers to other VA facilities) after receiving in-patient treatment for nonservice-connected conditions, with about 2,800 patients remaining in the facilities.

## PROCESSING TIMES

Processing times for claims averaged 112 days for veterans and 68 days for survivors during 1999, compared to Office of Management and Budget goals of 77 and 44 days, for these claims.

## 2001 COLA

In January, 2001, the target income levels upon which individual VA pension benefits are based increased by 3.5%, the same Cost of Living Adjustment (COLA) applied to Social Security and most other federal benefits.

*Chapter 5*

# MILITARY RETIREMENT

### *Robert L. Goldich*

## INTRODUCTION

The military retirement system includes benefits for retirement after an active or reserve military career, disability retirement, and survivor benefits for eligible survivors of deceased retirees.

The proposed change to the system that has generated the most recent legislative activity involves whether some or all military retirees should be allowed to receive both military retired pay and any VA disability compensation to which they are otherwise entitled; this is referred to as "concurrent receipt." A longer-term issue is whether some military personnel should be entitled to military retired pay with less than 20 years of service and whether many more personnel should serve well past the 20-year point before retiring. A recent DOD legislative proposal would make some changes along these lines for generals and admirals.

## Concurrent Receipt

Current law provides that military retired pay be reduced by the amount of VA disability compensation. Some maintain this is inequitable and unfair; it has been defended on grounds of cost and of the need to avoid setting a precedent for concurrent receipts of numerous other benefits.

The FY2003 National Defense Authorization Act authorized DOD payments to certain military retirees, either with (1) a Purple Heart indicating a combat wound and at least a 10% disability; or (2) at least a 60% disability, but not a wound leading to a Purple Heart, if the disability resulted from activity related to actual military operations (i.e., training, exercises, work performed on a military base or in a military environment, whether or not during actual hostilities). The result of the new benefit will be that eligible retirees will receive the financial equivalence of concurrent receipt, but in legal and statutory terms the concurrent receipt ban remains in effect. The new program, entitled "Combat Related Special Compensation," (CRSC), became effective May 31, 2003; information and application forms are available at two DOD websites, listed below.

The FY2004 Congressional Budget Resolution failed to adopt a Senate-passed provision that would have funded partial concurrent receipt, and there were no concurrent receipt related provisions in the initial House and Senate versions of the FY2004 National Defense Authorization Act. However, the Senate opened the bill to reconsideration of amendments, and a floor amendment by Senator Reid authorizing full concurrent receipt was passed on June 4. A discharge petition is being circulated in the House to bring a concurrent receipt bill to the floor. However, most observers think it likely that, as in 2002, the President will be opposed to, and be willing to veto any defense authorization bill containing, concurrent receipt.

## Changing the 20-Year Retirement Paradigm

Some argue that requiring military personnel to serve at least 20 years before retiring is inefficient and expensive. Others have argued that it is essential to maintaining a high-quality career force capable of meeting wartime requirements. Some changes along these lines, primarily for general and flag officers, are embodied in the DOD legislative proposal sent to Congress on April 10, 2003, entitled the "Defense Transformation for the 21st Century Act." Only a few of these changes were adopted in either the House or Senate versions of the FY2004

National Defense Authorization Act, however, and report language implies considerable skepticism about them in the Congress.

## MOST RECENT DEVELOPMENTS

On June 4, 2003, the Senate passed Senator Reid's floor amendment to the defense authorization bill to authorize full concurrent receipt, identical to similar amendments offered earlier and in past years. It passed by voice vote. (Although the Senate passed its version of the authorization bill on May 22, it reopened it to consideration of several amendments, of which concurrent receipt was one, on June 4.)

## BACKGROUND AND ANALYSIS

### Military Retirement: Key Elements and Issues Conceptual and Political Setting

Congress confronts both constituent concerns and budgetary constraints in considering military retirement issues. The approximately 2.0 million military retirees and survivor benefit recipients, and their roughly six to eight million family members, have been, and continue to be, an articulate and well-educated constituent group familiar with the legislative process and represented by associations staffed with military retirees with long experience in working with Congress. In recent years, the long-standing efforts by military retirees and their associations to secure more benefits for their members have been buttressed by (1) the outpouring of nation-wide nostalgia and support for the past heroism and current old-age needs of the "greatest generation" of World War II-era veterans, whether retirees or not; (2) concern over problems the military services were having in recruiting and retaining sufficient numbers of qualified personnel, which began in the mid-1990s, and the extent to which actual or perceived inadequacies in retirement benefits may have been contributing to these problems; (3) the impression by many current or former military personnel that the Clinton Administration was not favorably disposed toward the military as an institution, leading to efforts to portray increased retirement benefits as a palliative, and (4) in a reversal of the attitudes toward the Clinton Administration, efforts to obtain more benefits from the Bush Administration because it is perceived as being pro-military. And, since September 11, 2001, there has been a predictably dramatic increase in public and congressional support for the Armed Forces.

In addition, it can be posited that the policy choices posed by recently-enacted increased benefits for military retirees are an integral part of a larger debate in the United States over the distribution of pension-type resources among younger workers and older retirees. In the defense context, it may take the form of conflicts between DOD and current active duty and reserve military personnel on the one hand, with the responsibility of defending the United States in the present, and retired military personnel, many of whom feel that they are losing benefits to which they assumed they would always have access. On the other hand, it can be argued that, in a defense budget close to $400 billion yearly, benefits that cost the DOD budget only $7-8 billion yearly are not significant enough to force serious policy choices between current defense capability on the one hand, and, on the other, pensions for those who, despite their patriotic service, are not providing any current defense capability.

In general, in recent years Congress has been more aggressive than the executive branch in responding to the stated concerns of retirees about their benefits. The Department of Defense (DOD) and other executive branch agencies have, over time, tended to regard military retirement benefits as a place where substantial budgetary savings could be made. For instance, as noted below, Congress took the initiative in 1999 to repeal the "Redux" cuts in future military retired pay that was originally enacted in 1986.

## Program Summary

In FY2004, total federal budget outlays for military retirement will be an estimated $36.7 billion and DOD budget outlays will be an estimated $12.5 billion. (The differing figures for total federal and DOD outlays result from the use of the accrual method in accounting for the costs of military retirement. See the section below on *Cost Data* for a discussion of accrual accounting. These numbers, taken from **Table 2**, below, also differ slightly from those in **Table 1**, immediately below, for purely technical reasons without policy significance.) **Table 1** shows the estimated numbers of retirees, and the costs to the federal government of the retired pay they receive, for FY2002-FY2004.

## "Redux": Its 1986 Enactment and 1999 Repeal

Cuts in retired pay for future retirees were enacted in the Military Retirement Reform Act of 1986 (P.L. 99-348, July 1, 1986; the "1986 Act," now referred to frequently as the "Redux" military retirement system). Although enactment of Redux in 1986 represented a success for those who argued that the pre-Redux system was too generous, the repeal of compulsory Redux in late 1999 by the FY2000 National Defense Authorization Act indicated that, at least in Congress, those who defend the pre-Redux system are again ascendant.

**Table 1.** DOD Retired Military Personnel and Survivors: Estimated Numbers and Costs, FY2002-FY2004

|  | Total | Retirees from an Active Duty Military Career | Disability Retirees | Reserve Retirees | Survivor Benefit Recipients |
|---|---|---|---|---|---|
| FY2004 | 2,022,000/ $37.14 billion | 1,400,000/ $30.80 billion | 91,000/ $1.24 billion | 254,000/ $2.91 billion | 272,000/ $2.19 billion |
| FY2003 | 2,008,000/ $36.16 billion | 1,392,000/ $29.98 billion | 93,000/ $1.26 billion | 251,000/ $2.80 billion | 269,000/ $2.12 billion |
| FY2002 | 1,993,000/ $35.25 billion | 1,384,000/ $29.22 billion | 96,000/ $1.28 billion | 248,000/ $2.69 billion | 265,000/ $2.06 billion |

**Sources:** Office of the Actuary. Department of Defense. *Valuation of the Military Retirement System. September 30, 2001*: K-8, K-10, K-14, K-16, L-2, and L-4. Document available online from the Office of the DOD Actuary at [http://dod.mil/actuary/#].

Congress began taking notice publicly of potential problems related to Redux in 1997, well before the executive branch addressed the issue. During the fall of 1998, the Administration announced that it supported Redux repeal. Eventually, the FY2000 National Defense Authorization Act contained provisions for repealing compulsory Redux; it allows post-August 1, 1986 entrants to retire under the pre-Redux system or opt for Redux plus an immediate $30,000 cash payment(see below).

## Entitlement to Retired Pay and Retired Pay Computation Base

A service member becomes entitled to retired pay upon completion of 20 years of service, regardless of age. (The average nondisabled enlisted member retiring from an active duty military career in FY2001 was 42 years old and had 22 years of service; the average officer was 47 years old and had 24 years of service.) A member who retires from active duty is paid an immediate monthly annuity based on a percentage of his or her retired pay computation base. For persons who entered military service before September 8, 1980, the retired pay computation base is final monthly basic pay being received at the time of retirement. For those who entered service on or after September 8, 1980, the computation base is the average of the highest 3 years (36 months) of basic pay. (Basic pay is one component of total Regular Military Compensation, or RMC, which consists of basic pay, housing and subsistence allowances, and the federal tax advantage that accrues because the allowances are not taxable. Basic pay comprises approximately 70% of the total for all retirement eligibles: 75% for 30-year retirees and 66% for 20-year retirees. Thus, the 20- year retiree may get 50% of retired pay computation base upon retirement, but only 33% of RMC. The 30-year retiree will receive 75% of the computation base, but only 56% of RMC. Nor do any of these calculations include any of the many special pays, bonuses or other cash compensation to which many military members are entitled.)

## Retired Pay Computation Formula

### *Military Personnel Who First Entered the Service before August 1, 1986*

All military personnel who first entered military service *before* August 1, 1986, have their retired pay computed at the rate of 2.5% of the retired pay computation base for each year of service. The minimum amount of retired pay to which a member entitled to compute his or her retired pay under this formula is therefore 50% of the retired pay computation base (20 years of service X 2.5%). A 25-year retiree receives 62.5% of the computation base (25 years of service X 2.5%). The maximum, reached at the 30-year mark, is 75% of the computation base (30 years of service X 2.5%).

## *Military Personnel Who First Entered the Service on or after August 1, 1986*

Personnel who first enter service *on or after* August 1, 1986, in accordance with the provisions of the FY2000 National Defense Authorization Act, are required to select one of two options in calculating their retired pay within 180 days of reaching 15 years of service:

### Option 1: Pre-Redux

They can opt to have their retired pay computed in accordance with the pre-Redux formula, described above, but with a slightly modified COLA formula, which is less generous than that of the pre-Redux formula (see below, under COLAs).

### Option 2: Redux

They can opt to have their retired pay computed in accordance with the Redux formula and receive an immediate $30,000 cash bonus (which can actually be paid in several annual installments if the recipient so wishes, for tax purposes).

*The Redux Formula: Under Age 62 Retirees*

Redux is different from the previous formula in two major ways. First, for retirees under age 62, retired pay will be computed at the rate of 2.0% of the retired pay computation base for each year of service through 20, and 3.5% for each year of service from 21-30. Under this new formula, therefore, a 20-year retiree will receive 40% of his or her retired pay computation base upon retirement (20 years of service X 2.0%), and a 25-year retiree will receive 57.5% of the computation base [(20 years of service X 2.0%) + (5 years of service X 3.5%)]. A 30-year retiree, however, will continue to receive 75% of the retired pay computation base [(20 years of service X 2.0%) + (10 years of service X 3.5%)]. The changed formula, therefore, is "skewed" much more sharply in favor of the longer-serving military careerist, theoretically providing an incentive to remain on active duty longer before retiring.

*The Redux Formula: Retirees 62 and Older*

Second, when a retiree reaches age 62, his or her retired pay will be recomputed based on the old formula, a straight 2.5% of the retired pay computation base for each year of service. Thus, beginning at 62, the 20-year retiree receiving 40% of the computation base for retired pay, according to the new formula, will begin receiving 50% of his or her original computation base; the 25-year retiree's annuity will jump from 57.5% of the original computation base to 62.5%; and the 30-year retiree's annuity, already at 75% of the original computation base under both the old and new formulas, will not change. (Note: this change is an increase in monthly retired pay, not a lump sum at age 62.)

## Temporary Early Retirement Authority (TERA), 1992-2001 (FY1993-FY2001)

The FY1993 National Defense Authorization Act (Sec. 4403, P.L. 102-484) granted temporary authority (which expired on September 30, 2001) for the services to offer early retirements to personnel with more than 15 but less than 20 years of service. TERA retired pay was calculated in the usual ways except that there is an additional reduction of one percent for every year of service below 20. Part or all of this latter reduction could be restored if the retiree worked in specified public service jobs (such as law enforcement, firefighting, and education) during the period immediately following retirement, until the point at which the retiree would have reached the 20-year mark if he or she had remained in the service.

## Military Retired Pay and Social Security

Military personnel do not contribute a percentage of their salary to help pay for retirement benefits. They have paid taxes into the social security trust fund since January 1, 1957, and are entitled to full social security benefits based on their military service. Military retired pay and social security are not offset against each other; military retirees receive full social security benefits in addition to their military retired pay.

## Modifying 20-Year Retirement

For more than 30 years, the military retirement system, in particular, its central feature of allowing career personnel to retire at any age with an immediate annuity upon completing 20 years of service, has been the object of intense criticism and equally intense support among military personnel, politicians, and defense manpower analysts. Critics of the system have alleged, since its basic tenets were established by legislation enacted in the late 1940s, that it costs too much, has lavish benefits, and contributes to inefficient military personnel management by inducing too many personnel to stay until the 20-year mark and too few to stay beyond the 20-year mark. At present, they say, too few people are willing to make the commitment to stay the full 20 years, causing DOD to lose too many talented people in the 8-12 year range. In addition, the requirement for officers to perform a certain amount of joint (interservice) duty, plus acquiring a well-rounded competence in their own services' capabilities, has created a situation in which 20 years is simply not enough time for an officer to serve in enough jobs to learn all that is needed to prepare for higher command and staff duties. This allegedly shows a need for more officers to serve well past 20 years. In fact, the mandatory joint duty requirements are the only new factor in this issue, which has been an object of controversy since the late 1960s. Many analysts, however, feel that the joint duty requirements have, in connection with other duty required of an officer to attain a sufficient level of competence in his or her grade, simply made a 20-year career incapable of attainment — all of the service requirements cannot be "crammed into" 20 years.

Others have strongly defended the existing system as essential to recruiting and maintaining sufficient high-quality career military personnel who could withstand the rigors of arduous peacetime training and deployments as well as war. They tend to agree with the statement that "20-year retirement makes up with power what it lacks in subtlety," by providing a 20-year "pot of gold at the end of the rainbow." Without the latter, it is argued, too few personnel would be willing to put up with the great stresses of a military career. At the same time, the incentive to depart soon after reaching the 20-year mark supposedly prevents the armed forces from being saddled with over-age and unfit officers and NCOs, unquestionably a major problem in the early stages of both World Wars. Since 20-year retirement was adopted in the late 1940s, the latter problem has not surfaced when U.S. forces have been in combat. It is also suggested that DOD already has the tools to cope with the problems of insufficient retention of middle-grade personnel and with overloaded officer career patterns: the former by using special pays and bonuses and adequate overall military compensation and the latter by exercising existing discretionary authority in statute to keep more personnel on active duty well past the 20-year mark.

Secretary of Defense Rumsfeld and other senior defense officials have suggested on several occasions that the existing 20-year retirement paradigm should be modified. In general, though, they have cautioned, however, that they do not want to cause undue alarm, or negate individual career decisions already made, by introducing such changes too abruptly. Discussion about such "reforms" — that is, cuts — in retired pay entitlements was muted in the aftermath of the September 11, 2001 attacks. However, the proposed "Defense Transformation for the 21st Century Act," a legislative proposal sent to the Congress by DOD in late

April 2003, included, for the first time, provisions to allow the services to lengthen the maximum years of service of general and flag officers and be more flexible in their assignments. Specifically, the proposed Act would:

- extend the age limits for retirement of general/flag officers from the current 62 to 68, waiveable to 72 in some cases;

- eliminate mandatory retirement of general and flag officers after the current 30, 35, 38, and 40 years of service for, respectively, brigadier generals/rear admirals (lower half) (one-star officers; pay grade 0-7); major generals/rear admirals (two stars; pay grade 0-8); and lieutenant generals/vice admirals (three stars; pay grade 0-9); and full generals/admirals (four stars; pay grade 0-10);

- allow general and flag officers with more than 30 years of service to receive retired pay that is more than the current maximum of 75% of their retired pay computation base;

- eliminate a cap on the retired pay of general/flag officers, which results from the operation of laws that restrict active duty military basic pay; and

- reduce the number of years an officer in various grades would have to serve before being allowed to retire in that grade, for both general/flag officers and officers in grades 0-5 (lieutenant colonel/Navy commander) and 0-6 (colonel/Navy captain).

The net effects of these provisions would be to prevent the mandatory retirement of skilled high-level officers who might otherwise want to stay on active duty; give DOD and the military services more flexibility in managing the senior uniformed leadership of the services; allow generals and admirals to serve longer tours of duty and minimize too-frequent rotation of assignments; and provide greater compensation incentives related to the greater lengths of service. However, some opposed to them are concerned about longer terms for generals and admirals resulting in excessive stultification and stodginess in the senior uniformed leadership; an excessive slowing of promotions, as more people stay on active duty in the same grade for longer periods of time; and, combined with other measures in the proposed bill, a greater alignment of the senior generals and admirals with the senior appointed political leadership of DOD, and, hence, the Administration and political party in power. Only one of the categories of military personnel management changes noted above that were contained in this "Defense Transformation" legislative proposal was adopted in either the House or Senate versions of the FY2004 National Defense Authorization Act — specifically, the reduction in years in grade before an officer is allowed to retire in that grade.

## RETIRED PAY AND SURVIVOR BENEFIT COLAS

Military retired pay is protected against inflation by statute (10 USC 1401a). The Military Retirement Reform Act of 1986, in conjunction with recent changes in the FY2000 National Defense Authorization Act, provides for cost of living adjustments (COLAs) as indicated below. Congress has not modified the COLA formula since FY1996 (1995), although virtually every year since 1982 some COLA modifications, always with the aim of reducing costs and hence the payments to retirees, have been at least discussed. Therefore, it is probably inadvisable to assume at any time that COLAs will be totally off the table in future Congresses.

### What Was the Last COLA and What Will be the Next COLA?

The most recent military retirement COLA was **2.6%**, first applied to the retired pay disbursed on **January 1, 2002**. The most recent previous COLA was that of January 1, 2001, of 3.5%. The COLA which will become effective on **January 1, 2003**, will be **1.4%**, the second smallest since COLAs began in 1963 (the smallest were 1.3% in FY1998 and FY1986).

### COLAs for Pre-August 1, 1986 Entrants

For military personnel who first entered military service before August 1, 1986, each December a cost-of-living-adjustment (COLA) equal to the percentage increase in the Consumer Price Index (CPI) between the third quarters of successive years will be applied to military retired pay for the annuities paid beginning each January 1. For example, assume that the Consumer Price Index rises from 400.0 in September 2005 to 412.0 in September 2006, an increase of 12.0 points or 3.0% of 400.0. The monthly retired pay that accrues during December 2006, and will actually be paid to retirees on January 1, 2007, would be increased by 3.0% above that amount paid the previous month.

## COLAs for Personnel Who Entered Service On or After August 1, 1986

For those personnel who first entered military service on or after August 1, 1986, the FY2000 National Defense Authorization Act provides that their COLAs will be calculated in accordance with either of two methods, as noted below.

### *Non-Redux Recipients*

Those personnel who opt to have their retired pay computed in accordance with the pre-Redux formula will have their COLAs computed as described above for pre-August 1, 1986 entrants.

### *Redux/$30,000 Cash Bonus Recipients*

Those personnel who opt to have their retired pay computed in accordance with the Redux formula, and receive the $30,000 cash bonus, will have their COLAs computed as follows. Annual COLAs will be held to one percentage point below the actual inflation rate for retirees under age 62. Retirees covered by this new COLA formula would thus receive a 2.0% increase (rather than 3.0%) in their military retired pay under the hypothetical example described in the above paragraph. When a retiree reaches age 62, there will be a one-time recomputation of his or her annuity to make up for the lost purchasing power caused by the holding of COLAs to the inflation rate minus one percentage point. This recomputation will be applied to the old, generally more liberal retired pay computation formula on which retirees 62 or older will have their annuities computed. For most retirees, the size of this one-time annuity increase. After the recomputation at 62, however, future COLAs will continue to be computed on the basis of the inflation rate minus one percentage point.

### *Costs and Benefits of the Two Retirement Alternatives*

An analysis of the economic effects for hypothetical retirees indicates that in almost all cases opting for the pre- Redux formula will pay the individual much more over time. A report of the Center for Naval Analyses states that the more liberal retired pay computation formula and COLA formula of pre-Redux far outweighs the short-term benefits of a $30,000 pre-tax cash bonus. The report did say that it might be possible for an individual investor to "beat" these negative aspects of the bonus by wise investment decisions but that it would be difficult. Naturally, no study can know what an individual's financial situation is. At first, only a fairly small percentage of personnel opted for the $30,000 lump sum.

However, the proportion has been rising, despite the fact that in virtually all cases it provides less money in the long run.

## MILITARY RETIREMENT BUDGETING AND COSTS

### Accounting for Military Retirement in the Federal Budget

All DOD budgets through FY1984 reflected the costs of retired pay actually being paid out to personnel who had already retired. Congress simply appropriated the amount of money required to pay current retirees each year. Since FY1985, the "accrual accounting" concept has been used to budget for the costs of military retired pay. Under this system, the DOD budget for each fiscal year reflects the estimated amount of money that must be set aside and accrued at interest from investment in special, non-marketable U.S. government securities similar in some ways to Treasury bills and bonds. This interest funds the retired pay to which persons currently in the Armed Forces during that fiscal year, and who ultimately retire, will be entitled in the future. These estimated future retirement costs are arrived at by making projections based on the past rates at which active duty military personnel stayed in the service until retirement, and on assumptions regarding the overall U.S. economy, such as interest rates, inflation rates, and military pay levels. These DOD budget outlays for retirement are computed as a percentage of a fiscal year's total military pay costs for each military service. Approximately 35-40% of military basic pay costs must be added to the DOD personnel budget each fiscal year to cover the future retirement costs of those personnel who ultimately retire from the military.

*DOD budget outlays* in each fiscal year that pay for the estimated cost of future retirees are transferred in a paper transaction to a Military Retirement Fund, located in the Income Security Function of the federal budget. The Military Retirement Fund also receives [paper] transfers from the General Fund of the Treasury to fund the initial unfunded liability of the military retirement system. This is the total future cost of military retired pay that will result from military service performed prior to the implementation of accrual accounting in FY1985. Money is disbursed from this Military Retirement Fund to current retirees. Individual retirees continue to receive their retired pay from DOD finance centers. Technically, however, because this money paid to individuals comes not from the DOD budget, but from the Fund, it is paid out by the Income Security function of the federal budget. Actual payments to current retirees thus show up in the federal budget as outlays from the federal budget as a whole, but not from DOD. Under accrual accounting, therefore, total federal outlays for each fiscal year continue to reflect only costs of payments to military members who have already retired, as was the case before accrual accounting began. Accrual accounting only changes the manner in which the federal government accounts for military retired pay; it does not affect actual payments to individuals in any way.

## Unfunded Liability

Current debates over both federal civilian and military retirement have included some discussion of the "unfunded liability" of both. As noted above, the military retirement system's unfunded liability consists of future retired pay costs incurred before the creation of the Military Retirement Fund in FY1985. These obligations are being liquidated by the payment to the Fund each year of an amount from the General Fund of the Treasury, and will be fully paid, based on current calculations, by FY2033. The unfunded liability at the end of FY2001 was $539.6 billion; the estimated liability for FY2002 was $555.2 billion; for FY2003, $570.1 billion; and for FY2004, $586.7 billion.

Some concerns have been voiced about the amount of unfunded liability. However, (1) the hundreds of billions of dollars of unfunded liability is a cumulative amount to be paid to retirees over the next 50 years, not all at once; (2) by the time some persons first become eligible for retired pay under the pre-accrual accounting system, many others will have died; and (3) unlike the private sector, there is no way for employees to claim immediate payment of their future benefits. An analogy would be that most homeowners cannot afford to pay cash for a house, so they get a mortgage. If the mortgage had to be paid in full, almost no homeowners could afford to do so. However, spread out over 30 years, the payments are affordable. Similarly, the unfunded liability of federal retirement programs is affordable when federal retirement outlays are spread over many decades.

## Military Retirement Cost Trends

Because military retirement is an entitlement, rather than a discretionary program, its costs to the *total federal budget* (payments to current retirees and survivors) always rise modestly each year, due to a predictable slow rise in the number of retirees and survivors. The cost to DOD (estimated future retirement costs of current personnel) declined after FY1989 (the beginning of the post-Cold War drawdown), as the size of the force, and therefore the number of people who will retire from it in the future, declined. However, as the drawdown stabilized, so did the DOD budget costs of retirement. **Table 2** indicates the costs of military retired pay in federal budget outlays (payments to current retirees) and Department of Defense accrual outlays (money set aside to fund future retirees).

Table 2. Military Retirement Outlays
(billions of current dollars)

|  | Total Federal Budget Outlays | Accrual Outlays from DOD Budget |
|---|---|---|
| Estimated FY2004* | $36.7 | $12.5 |
| Estimated FY2003* | 35.9 | 12.1 |
| Actual FY2002* | 35.1 | 12.9 |
| Actual FY2001** | 34.1 | 11.4 |
| Actual FY2000** | 32.9 | 11.6 |

*FY2004 Budget of the United States Government. Appendix: 859.
**FY2003 Budget of the United States Government. Appendix: 903.

# CONCURRENT RECEIPT OF MILITARY RETIRED PAY AND VA DISABILITY COMPENSATION

## Military Retired Pay and VA Disability Compensation: Current Situation

Most people familiar with military retirement would probably agree that the most controversial military retirement issue that is currently the object of intense congressional interest is that involving concurrent receipt of military retired pay and Department of Veterans' Affairs (VA) disability compensation. Current law requires that military retired pay be reduced by the amount of any VA disability compensation received. For several years some military retirees have sought a change in law to permit receipt of all or some of both, and legislation to allow this has been introduced during the past several Congresses, frequently having co-sponsors well above half of both the House and the Senate. This issue is frequently referred to as "concurrent receipt," because it would involve the simultaneous receipt of two types of benefits. In 1999, legislation was enacted to provide "special compensation" to certain severely disabled military retirees who would be eligible for concurrent receipt if concurrent receipt were ever enacted; in 2002, further legislation, known as "combat-related special compensation," or CSRC, was enacted that provides, for certain seriously disabled retirees, a cash benefit financially identical to what concurrent receipt would provide them. Neither type of "special compensation" removed the statutory prohibition on actual concurrent receipt.

The George W. Bush Administration (and the Clinton Administration before it) has been consistently opposed to concurrent receipt. The Bush Administration had threatened to veto the FY2003 National Defense Authorization Act if the Act included a concurrent receipt provision. It did agree, obviously, to the quasi-concurrent receipt provision of the FY2003 National Defense Authorization Act, signed by the President on December 2, 2002 (see below).

## *VA Disability Compensation*

To qualify for VA disability compensation, a determination must be made by the VA that the veteran sustained a particular injury or disease, or had a preexisting condition aggravated, while serving in the Armed Forces. Some exceptions exist for certain conditions that may not have been apparent during military service but which are presumed to have been service-connected. The VA has a scale of 10 ratings, from 10% to 100%, although there is no special arithmetic relationship between the amount of money paid for each step. Each percentage rating entitles the veteran to a specific level of disability compensation. In a major difference from the DOD disability retirement system, a veteran receiving VA disability compensation can ask for a medical reexamination at any time (or a veteran who does not receive disability compensation upon separation from service can be reexamined later). All VA disability compensation is tax-free, which makes receipt of VA compensation desirable, even with the operation of the offset.

## *Interaction of DOD and VA Disability Benefits*

Military disability retirees, as well as retirees not determined disabled by DOD, can also apply to the VA for disability compensation. This can be advantageous to retirees who have a DOD disability rating. For instance, a retiree whose retired pay is offset by the retiree's VA compensation nonetheless receives some advantage because the VA compensation is totally tax-free. Also, a retiree may (1) apply for VA compensation any time after leaving the service and (2) have his or her degree of disability changed by the VA as the result of a later medical reevaluation, as noted above. Many retirees seek benefits from the VA years after retirement for a condition that may have been incurred during military service but that does not manifest itself until many years later.

## *Military Disability Retirement*

To qualify for military disability retirement, a military member must be certified as permanently disabled by a DOD medical examination. The individual must have (1) at least 20 years of service, **or** (2) a disability of at least 30% *and* have a disability incurred on active duty. That is, personnel with a disability rated at 30% or more by DOD, but who have less than 20 years of service, can be retired on disability (there is no minimum limit). Similarly, personnel with disability of less than 30% can be retired on disability as long as their disabling condition was incurred while on active duty. Disability retired pay is computed on the basis of one of two formulae, whichever is more advantageous to the individual: (1) the non-disability formula described above, or (2) the retired pay computation base multiplied by the percentage of disability. DOD makes a determination of eligibility for disability retirement only once, at the time the individual is separating from the service. Although DOD uses the VA schedule of types of disabilities to determine the percentage of disability, DOD measures disability, or lack thereof, against the extent to which the individual can or cannot perform military duties, rather than his or her ability to perform post-service civilian work. A military retiree, regardless of his or her DOD disability status immediately upon retirement, can apply for VA disability compensation at any time after leaving active military duty. Military disability retired pay is usually taxable, unless related to a combat disability.

## "Special Compensation" For Severely Disabled Retirees

The **FY2000, FY2001, and FY2002 National Defense Authorization Acts** authorized what was, in effect, *de facto* concurrent receipt for severely disabled military retirees, known in statute as "special compensation." In FY2003, monthly payments of $50 are authorized for retirees, both disability and nondisability, with 60% VA disability; $100 for 70% disabled retirees; $125 for 80%; $225 for 90%; and $325 for 100% VA disabled retirees, if the disability rating was received from the VA within 4 years of retiring from military service. This compensation is limited by its statute to retired personnel with at least 20 years of service. It therefore is not available to retirees who retired with less than 20 years of service in accordance with the Temporary Early Retirement Authority (TERA) in effect during 1992-2001 (FY1993-FY2001) or with any disability retiree with less than 20 years of active duty. [10 USC 1413(c)(1)].

On **October 1, 2004**, the dollar amounts will rise further to $125 for 70%, $150 for 80%, $250 for 90%, and $350 for 100%. (Sec.641 of the FY2002 Act). Eligible personnel need not apply for the pay; their eligibility is identified by DOD and VA computers automatically. About 20,000 retirees qualified for these special payments as defined in the FY2000 and FY2001 laws; it is not yet clear how many additional individuals will be added to the roll of eligibles by the FY2002 Act, although it will be no more than 23,000 (the current number of 60% disabled retirees). The "quasi-concurrent receipt" provisions contained in the FY2003 defense authorization act, discussed in detail below, do not effect this special compensation, except that retirees will not be allowed to receive both types of special compensation; they will be allowed to pick whichever one they find most financially advantageous.

## "COMBAT RELATED SPECIAL COMPENSATION" (CSRC) FOR CERTAIN DISABLED RETIREES

On December 2, 2002, the President signed the FY2003 National Defense Authorization Act (P.L. 107-314; 116 Stat. 2458). This followed the House and Senate approval, on November 12, 2002, of the conference report (H.Rept. 107-436) on this Act. Section 636 of the conference bill contains concurrent-receipt-generated provisions. Section 636 provides for a new category of DOD "special compensation" for certain military retirees. This benefit, entitled "Combat Related Special Compensation," or CRSC, by DOD, is available to military retirees who have at least 20 years of service and who have *either*:

- A disability that is "attributable to an injury for which the member was awarded the Purple Heart," and is not rated as less than a 10% disability by DOD or the VA; *or*

- At least a 60% disability rating from either DOD or the VA, incurred due to involvement in "armed conflict," "hazardous service," "duty simulating war," and "through an instrumentality of war." This appears, in lay terms, to encompass combat with any kind of hostile force; hazardous duty such as diving, parachuting, using dangerous materials such as explosives, and the like; individual training and unit training and exercises and maneuvers in the field; and "instrumentalities of war" such as accidents in combat vehicles or, if due to training-related activities, aboard naval vessels or military aircraft, and accidental injuries due to occurrences such as munitions explosions, injuries from gases or vapors related to training for combat, and the like.

The payments will be equal to the amount of VA disability compensation to which the retiree is entitled, but the new legislation does *not* end the requirement that the retiree's military retired pay be reduced by whatever VA compensation to which the retiree is entitled.

Under the new law, therefore, the eligible retirees will receive the financial equivalence of concurrent receipt, but in legal and statutory terms it will *not* constitute concurrent receipt, and the statute also states that it explicitly is *not* retired pay *per se*. In addition, the law provides that any retiree eligible for this new special compensation will not be entitled to the existing special compensation first established in 2000 for potentially concurrent-receipt eligible retirees.

Military *nondisability* retirees (those who do not retire from DOD based on any disability) may be eligible for this combat-disability special compensation, if they receive a VA disability rating [see subsection 1413a (e)(1)(B)(ii) of title 10, as enacted in the new law]. As noted above, the VA and the DOD disability determination processes are independent of each other. Military *disability* retirees will be entitled to this new combat disability special compensation under specific circumstances. If they were retired for disability but were also entitled to have their retired pay computed on the basis of the nondisability formula (i.e., had at least 20 years of service in most cases), they will be entitled to any amount of the new special compensation to which the VA disability determination would entitle them, with one important exception. This latter exception would apply to retirees whose disability was so severe that having their retired pay computed in accordance with the percentage of disability would actually give them more money than if it were computed on the basis of their 20 years or more of service. For these retirees, their special compensation would be reduced by the difference between the two formulas. This is done on the assumption that to give them the extra due to disability, together with the VA disability compensation, would in fact be doing what the opponents of concurrent receipt have argued: giving a person two types of compensation for the same disability. The determination as to whether a retiree's disability is "combat-related" in accordance with the new statute will be made by DOD.

According to news reports, DOD has decided on a preliminary basis that the CSRC payments should *not* be subject to federal income tax.

This new entitlement became effective May 31, 2003, just meeting the deadline of 180 days after enactment contained in the FY2003 Act; i.e., June 2, 2003. DOD had to wrestle with the complex issues involved in defining exactly what kind of disabilities meet the criterion of combat-related other than those that can be directly attributed to receipt of a Purple Heart. According to DOD, "Payments for qualified retirees will accrue beginning June 1 [2003] with first payments possible on July 1 [2003]." Retirees will be "grandfathered" regarding the legislation; individuals who are already retired will be allowed to apply for the new benefit. Applications and information are available on two DOD web sites: [https://www.dmdc.osd.mil/crsc] or [http://web1.whs.osd.mil/ichome/ddeforms.htm]. Retirees may also phone the retirement services offices of their service for the necessary information.

Certain aspects of the CSRC may receive legislative attention in the 108th Congress. First, DOD has interpreted the new law as requiring the payment of the special compensation based on the disability compensation received by a veteran without regard to the veteran's dependents. The rate for a disabled veteran with a spouse, dependent child, and/or dependent parents is higher. Hence, the continued prohibition on actual concurrent receipt will require the "with dependents" rate to be deducted from the military retiree's DOD retired pay, but the CSRC will replace this loss with only the lesser rate for a veteran without dependents. Second, DOD has interpreted the law as requiring reserve retirees to have at least 7,200 reserve retirement "points" to be eligible for CSRC. A reservist receives a certain number of retirement points for varying levels of participation in the reserves, or active duty military service. This is an extraordinarily high point level — in fact, it could only be attained by a reservist who had at least 20 years of *active duty* military service. However, the CSRC statute authorizes CSRC to be paid only to retirees with at least 20 years of service; hence, DOD feels it has no choice to require the equivalent of 20 years from reservists. The reserve and National Guard community may well seek to have this aspect of CSRC modified.

## Concurrent Receipt Legislation in the 108th Congress

### *108th Congress Concurrent Receipt Action Now Seems Unlikely*

It seemed virtually certain at the end of 2002 that concurrent receipt would be the object of intense legislative interest in the 108th Congress. The organized military retiree community had stated its dissatisfaction with the new "special compensation" enacted in the FY2003 National Defense Authorization Act, arguing that it provides a small benefit to a small number of retirees and, perhaps more importantly, leaves the statutory ban on concurrent receipt intact. At the same time, there was, and is, no indication that the Administration would be inclined to drop its strong opposition to repealing the concurrent receipt ban, up to and including a veto threat, as was the case with the FY2003 bill. However, the Iraq war and the concern over related military benefit matters appears, to a considerable degree, to have "crowded out" military compensation legislation not more related to active duty military and the reserve components, although efforts are under way to force concurrent receipt to the floor of both the House and Senate.

### *FY2004 Congressional Budget Resolution*

The conference report on the FY2004 congressional budget resolution, reported on April 11, 2003, did *not* include a Senate provision allotting money for partial concurrent receipt in FY2004. The lack of provision in the budget resolution for any kind of concurrent receipt was a first indication, based on congressional action, of the probable lack of significant movement toward congressional action on concurrent receipt during 2003.

Previously, on March 25, the Senate had approved a floor amendment to its version of the FY2004 budget resolution offered by Senator Harry Reid, which would fund partial concurrent receipt for the period FY2004-FY2013. The "partial" nature of the concurrent receipt assumed in the amendment was twofold: it would have been limited to military retirees with at least a 60% service-connected disability; and it would have been phased in over the three-year period calendar year 2004 through calendar year 2006. In 2004, only 40% of the retired pay to which the beneficiaries would otherwise be entitled would have been paid out; in 2005, 60%; in 2006, 80%, and 100% only in calendar year 2007. Another amendment by Senator Reid that would have funded full concurrent receipt was submitted for printing on March 20, 2003 (S.Amdt. 342), but never actually proposed.

### *FY2004 National Defense Authorization Act/Armed Services Committees*

On May 9 and May 14, 2003, the Senate and House Armed Services Committees, respectively, released their versions of the FY2004 National Defense Authorization Act. Neither bill, in a significant departure from recent previous years, contained any provisions related to concurrent receipt. On May 22, 2003, both houses passed their versions of the Act, with no change in the authorizing committees' lack of concurrent receipt provisions. The Senate reopened the authorization bill for amendments on June 4, and on that date, Senator Reid's floor amendment to authorize full concurrent receipt, identical to similar amendments offered earlier and in past years, was passed by voice vote. In addition, a discharge petition is being circulated in the House to bring to bring to the House floor H.R. 303, which would authorize full concurrent receipt on a basis identical to that of Senator Reid's floor amendment.

However, most observers feel that, as was the case in 2002 during consideration of the FY2003 National Defense Authorization Act, the President will state his intention to veto any defense authorization bill that contains a concurrent receipt provision. This eventually forced Congress to abandon attempts to enact actual concurrent receipt in 2002 and, instead, create the CRSC. There is no way of knowing at this time how the issue may be resolved in 2003.

## Costs of Concurrent Receipt

According to the most recent Congressional Budget Office (CBO) estimates, full concurrent receipt would cost approximately $3 billion in FY2004, rising to $5 billion by FY2013, and totaling $41 billion over the ten-year period FY2004-FY2013. Almost 700,000 retirees will be eligible in FY2004.

### *Costs of "Special Compensation" for Severely Disabled Retirees Enacted in 1999-2001 (FY2000-FY2002)*

CBO estimates that the "special compensation" enacted in the FY2000-2002 defense authorization acts would cost approximately $710 million over the period FY2003-FY2012. About 36,000 retirees are currently eligible.

### *Costs of the New "Combat Related Special Compensation (CRSC)" Enacted in 2002 (FY2003)*

Cost estimates for the CRSC vary widely, because estimates of the number of eligible beneficiaries and variables that will have to be settled by DOD's implementing regulations also vary. The most recent estimates of the cost during its first full year of operation, FY2004, vary considerably. CBO estimates $265 million (18,000 eligibles); the Office of Management and Budget (OMB), $269 million (no eligibles estimate); and DOD, $326 million (33,300 eligibles). Long-term cost estimates over the period FY2003-FY2012 vary as well. CBO projects about $6.0 billion; DOD, $3.7 billion; and OMB, $2.7 billion.

## Pros and Cons of Concurrent Receipt
These are only the most frequently cited positions on the issue.

## Major Arguments IN FAVOR of Concurrent Receipt

1) Military retired pay, was earned for length of service, the VA disability compensation, for disability. They were therefore for two different things and did not constitute a duplication of benefits.

2) If cost was an issue, partial concurrent receipt should be allowed for those most severely disabled, with combat disability, or whose benefits or total income are the least.

3) VA disability compensation beneficiaries are entitled to other federal benefits; why not military retired pay?

4) People receiving VA disability compensation can receive pensions from a wide variety of other sources without any offset; why target military retirees?

## Major Arguments AGAINST Concurrent Receipt

1) The cost of full, or nearly full, concurrent receipt would be enormous — some estimates say almost $5 billion yearly.

2) Eliminating or reducing this offset would "be sticking the camel's nose into the tent," setting a precedent for the reduction or elimination of all kinds of similar offsets of one or more federal payments, possibly costing billions of dollars.

3) Concurrent receipt could result in some individuals getting a new VA medical evaluation, resulting in a higher disability rating and hence eligibility for concurrent receipt benefits, or getting a VA evaluation when they had hitherto not done so. Both results would lead to more people getting VA compensation for the first time or higher amounts of it.

4) Although some federal programs do not have an offset against VA disability compensation, there are no such offsets involving disability and retirement from the same job and agency where the disability occurred.

5) VA disability compensation is supposedly authorized much more liberally than military disability retired pay, and a VA disability can be certified many years after a person leaves active military service. Concurrent receipt could lead to a windfall for people whose VA disability might have had a tenuous connection with their military service.

6) Concurrent receipt was never promised to those asking for it.

*Chapter 6*

# MILITARY TECHNICIANS: THE ISSUE OF MANDATORY RETIREMENT FOR NON-DUAL STATUS TECHNICIANS

### *Lawrence Kapp*

## INTRODUCTION

The National Defense Authorization Act for Fiscal Year 2000[1] contains policy changes affecting many U.S. military technicians, most notably a provision which mandates the retirement of certain retirement-eligible technicians. Under this legislation, Army and Air Force Reserve technicians who do not hold dual status and who are eligible for an "unreduced annuity" will be required to retire; if they do not hold dual status but are not yet eligible for an "unreduced annuity," they *may* be allowed, at the discretion of their respective service, to continue working until they become eligible for one, at which time they will be required to retire. Although Congress has settled the question for now, advocates for some military technicians argue that the policy should be repealed or modified.

This report will describe the duties of military technicians and the history of military technician programs in the National Guard, Army Reserve, and Air Force Reserve. It will outline the importance of the "dual status" requirement in these three distinct technician programs, explain the interest of Congress in this requirement, and recount the legislative attempts to strengthen its application. Finally, this report will discuss the stated rationale for the recently enacted mandatory retirement provision, linking it to Congress's past efforts to strengthen the dual status requirement, and assess the impact of this provision on military technicians.

## WHAT IS A MILITARY TECHNICIAN?

The reserve component[2] (RC) of the United States armed forces employs a small core group of full time employees to administer RC units, train RC personnel, and maintain RC equipment. These employees are known as Full-Time Support (FTS) personnel. There are four distinct types of FTS personnel: civilian employees, active duty military personnel, Active Guard and Reserve (AGR) personnel, and military technicians.[3] Military technicians are federal civilian employees, hired under statutes contained in titles 5 and 32, U.S. Code, who provide support primarily to wartime deployable units of the Selected Reserve.[4] Unlike regular civilian employees, however, military technicians are generally required to maintain membership in the Selected Reserve as a condition of their employment. They may also be required to fulfill their reserve obligation (i.e., drilling one weekend a month and attending two weeks of annual training) in the same unit they work for in their civilian capacity.[5] The principal intent of this

---

[1] P. L. 106-65; October 5, 1999.
[2] The reserve component of the United States military includes the Army Reserve, Navy Reserve, Air Force Reserve, Marine Corps Reserve, Coast Guard Reserve, Army National Guard, and the Air National Guard.
[3] Military technicians have also been referred to as "reserve technicians," "civilian technicians," "dual status technicians," "technicians" and "caretakers and clerks" in the past. The term used in the most recent federal legislation has been "military technicians" and is the terminology generally used throughout this paper. The term "technicians," however, is sometimes used as an abbreviation. It should be considered synonymous with the term "military technicians" unless stated otherwise.
[4] The Selected Reserve, a sub-element of the Ready Reserve, contains those units and individuals most essential to wartime missions. Members of the Selected Reserve generally perform, at a minimum, one weekend of training each month, and two weeks of training each year, for which they receive pay and benefits.
[5] A "unit membership requirement" for certain military technicians was enacted November 18, 1997, as part of P. L. 105-85 and is codified in Title 10, U.S. Code, section 10216 (d). Similar unit membership requirements have existed for many years within the administrative agreements which govern the military technician programs in the Army Reserve and the Air Force Reserve. In the case of the Army Reserve, the annual Department of Defense Appropriations Acts from FY1984 through FY1996 also contained language barring funds to certain technicians who did not hold reserve

policy is to guarantee that when a reserve unit is mobilized, the technicians who support it will be mobilized as well. This ensures that the expertise and skills of the technician workforce remain available to the unit when it needs them most.

Military technicians who hold membership in the Selected Reserve are referred to as "dual status technicians" because of their status as both civilian employees and reservists. However, for a variety of reasons which will be discussed later, not all military technicians belong to the Selected Reserve. These technicians are referred to as "non-dual-status technicians."[6] Precisely because they are not members of the Selected Reserve, non-dual-status technicians *cannot* be ordered to deploy with their unit when it is mobilized.[7] Thus, the supported unit is largely deprived of the technician's expertise and skills during its deployment.

## ORIGIN AND EVOLUTION OF THE MILITARY TECHNICIAN PROGRAM

As a federal program, the military technician program is over 80 years old and its history is fairly complex. The following section provides a brief overview of the program's origin and evolution. A more detailed account is contained in Appendix A of this report.

Military technicians are descended from the personnel described in Section 90 of the National Defense Act of 1916.[8] This act authorized the use of federal funds "for the compensation of competent help" to take care of the "material, animals, and equipment" in National Guard units. Subsequent legislation renamed the "competent help" as "caretakers and clerks." Until 1968, these "caretakers and clerks" were state employees, governed by state laws, but paid with federal funds. In 1968, however, Congress passed the National Guard Technicians Act,[9] which converted all "caretakers and clerks" from state employees to federal employees and renamed them "technicians."

---

membership in the same unit which they worked for in their civilian capacity. See footnote 63 for a full listing of these provisions.
[6] They are also sometimes referred to as "status quo" technicians.
[7] Non-dual-status technicians may *volunteer* to deploy with their units, as some did during the Gulf War, but they are under no obligation to do so.
[8] Statutes at Large, June 3, 1916, chapter 134, section 90.
[9] P. L. 90-486; 82 Stat. 755; August 13, 1968.

The Air Force Reserve and the Army Reserve established technician programs similar to the National Guard's in 1957 and 1960, respectively.[10] However, unlike the National Guard program, which was established by federal law, the Reserve programs were established administratively, under the broader statutory umbrella of the federal civil service. As such, the Reserve technician programs differed substantially from the National Guard program. Furthermore, because the Reserve technician programs operated under the authority of federal civil service laws, the Air Force Reserve and the Army Reserve needed the approval of the Civil Service Commission (now the Office of Personnel Management) before they could establish their technician programs. To win this approval, the Air Force Reserve and the Army Reserve each had to negotiate an agreement with the Civil Service Commission concerning employment conditions for the technicians. These agreements were negotiated separately and, as a result, the Air Force Reserve technician program differed substantially from the Army Reserve technician program.

One of the key differences among these three military technician programs – National Guard, Air Force Reserve, and Army Reserve – lies in the degree to which they required their technicians to maintain "dual status." A strict "dual status" provision would require military technicians to maintain membership in the Selected Reserve as a condition of their employment, usually in the same unit they work for in their civilian capacity. A less strict provision might make exceptions in certain cases, or merely encourage "dual status" while not requiring it.

Of the three military technician programs, the Army Reserve had the weakest dual status requirement.[11] The effect of this weaker "dual status" requirement was to create a technician program in the Army Reserve with a relatively high number of non-dual-status technicians. This eventually attracted the attention of Congress, which was concerned that the Army Reserve's readiness was being degraded by the presence of so many technicians who could not be required to deploy with their units in the case of mobilization.

---

[10] The Naval Reserve, Marine Corps Reserve, or the Coast Guard Reserve have never had a military technician program.
[11] For a comparison of dual-status requirements of the three programs, see Appendix A.

## CONGRESS AND THE DUAL STATUS REQUIREMENT: PAST LEGISLATIVE PROVISIONS

From 1983 to 1995, Congress repeatedly included provisions in defense appropriations bills aimed at reducing the numbers of non-dual-status technicians within the Army Reserve's military technician program. Yet, in spite of these efforts, the composition of the Army Reserve's technician workforce did not change appreciably. (For a detailed history of these legislative efforts and their impact see Appendix B). As a result, beginning in 1995, Congress began to take a broader and more aggressive approach towards managing the military technician workforce.

In 1995, Congress included a provision in the National Defense Authorization Act for Fiscal Year 1996 which established a strict dual-status requirement for all newly hired technicians, whether in the Army Reserve, the Air Force Reserve, or the National Guard.[12] Two years later, the National Defense Authorization Act for Fiscal Year 1998 contained several provisions related to military technicians and the "dual status" requirement. Specifically, it placed a limit on the number of non-dual-status technicians that could be employed in each of the technician programs and required the Secretary of Defense to submit a report to Congress outlining "a plan for ensuring that, on and after September 30, 2007, all military technician positions are held only by military technicians (dual status)."[13] The clear implication of this latter provision was that Congress was interested in phasing out the employment of all non-dual status technicians and wanted advice from the Department of Defense on how to accomplish this objective.

The Department of Defense submitted a report to Congress in 1999 which contained a plan to ensure that only dual-status technicians held military technician positions by the end of FY2007; however, the report raised a number of concerns about the fairness and feasibility of doing so. With respect to fairness, the report predicted that meeting the 2007 deadline would require DoD to involuntarily separate 2,655 non-dual-status technicians, many of whom would not be eligible for civil service retirement when separated.[14] Forced reductions of this sort, the DoD report argued, were unfair to the individual technicians:

---

[12] P. L. 104-106, section 513(c); 110 Stat. 306; February 10, 1996.
[13] P. L. 105-85, section 523; 111 Stat. 1737; November 18, 1997. The caps on the number of non-dual-status technicians which could be employed by the other Reserve organizations were as follows: 1,500 non-dual-status technicians in the Army Reserve; 2,400 in the Army National Guard; 450 in the Air National Guard; and zero in the Air Force Reserve by the end of fiscal year 1998.
[14] Department of Defense, Office of the Assistant Secretary of Defense for Reserve Affairs, "A Plan for Full Utilization of Military Technicians (Dual Status)," August 2, 1999, pages 7 and 8. Numbers

...non-dual status military technicians were hired and are managed according to various Reserve component policies. Non-dual status military technicians had a reasonable expectation that their positions carried career potential. The Department feels a moral obligation to recognize previous commitments and reasonable individual career expectations and to avoid forced reductions to the extent practicable.[15]

Another significant point raised in the DoD report dealt with the limited need for non-dual-status technicians in the National Guard. National Guard units usually operate under the authority of the Governor of the state or territory in which they are located. Each state or territory maintains a headquarters to oversee its units and military technicians are frequently employed in these headquarters. If these technicians hold dual-status, then they could potentially be mobilized by the federal government in times of national emergency and deployed with the unit they maintain membership in. This, DoD contended, could cripple the ability of the state headquarters to carry out its own important mission. "The National Guard," the report concluded, "cannot operate without a workforce that includes some employees who do not have to mobilize with the units they support." From this perspective, the National Guard has a bona fide need for at least some non-dual-status technicians.[16]

# CONGRESS AND THE DUAL STATUS REQUIREMENT: LEGISLATIVE PROVISIONS IN THE NATIONAL DEFENSE AUTHORIZATION ACT FOR FY2000, INCLUDING THE MANDATORY RETIREMENT PROVISIONS

As a result of the concerns raised by the Department of Defense, Congress substantially modified the idea of simply filling all military technician positions with dual-status technicians by 2007. The National Defense Authorization Act for FY2000 contains a new initiative which attempts to reconcile the desire of

---

are derived from the estimated Reductions in Force (RIFs) required by September 30, 2007, without benefit of additional retirement incentives.

[15] Department of Defense, Office of the Assistant Secretary of Defense for Reserve Affairs, "A Plan for Full Utilization of Military Technicians (Dual Status)," August 2, 1999, page 3

[16] A similar argument has been made by some military technicians with respect to the Army Reserve. A small proportion of Army Reserve military technicians are assigned to nondeploying headquarters units where they perform functions similar to those performed by a National Guard state headquarters. (At present, 558 military technicians, or 9% of the Army Reserve's technician workforce, fit this description). Thus, they argue, if the National Guard has a bona fide need for some non-dual-status technicians in its headquarters units, so too does the Army Reserve.

Congress to have an all dual-status technician workforce with the issues of fairness and necessity raised by the Department of Defense. With regards to the issue of necessity raised by the National Guard, the congressional response was fairly straightforward: the act authorized the National Guard to employ up to 1,950 non-dual-status technicians on and after October 1, 2001.[17]

Reconciling Congress's desire to have a dual-status technician workforce with the desire to treat non-dual-status technicians fairly, however, was a more complicated issue and the relevant legislation was therefore more complex. The issue is addressed in Section 522 of the National Defense Authorization Act for FY2000, first by categorizing military technicians – in the Army and Air Force Reserves only[18] – in two separate ways. First, it categorized technicians based on the date they were hired: "on or before" or "after" February 10, 1996, the date of enactment of the National Defense Authorization Act for FY1996. This distinguishes between those technicians who were hired when there was an ambiguous dual-status requirement, and those who were hired after a firm dual-status requirement had been codified into law. Second, it categorized them based on whether or not they held dual-status on October 5, 1999, the date on which the National Defense Authorization Act for FY2000 was enacted into law. This provision was principally administrative: it facilitated distinguishing those technicians who would be affected immediately and those who might be affected in the future. These two dividing lines produce four distinct categories of Army and Air Force Reserve military technicians: (1) those who were hired on or before February 10, 1996, and who held dual-status on October 5, 1999; (2) those who were hired on or before February 10, 1996 and who did not hold dual-status on October 5, 1999; (3) those who were hired after February 10, 1996, and who held dual-status on October 5, 1999; and (4) those who were hired after February 10, 1996, and who did not hold dual-status on October 5, 1999. The legislative provisions contained in Section 522 and a description of how they impact each of these four groups are discussed below. (These provisions and their impact are summarized in Table 1).

---

[17] P. L. 106-65, section 523; October 5, 1999. This figure represents about 4% of the total number of technicians currently authorized for the National Guard.
[18] The National Guard was not included in this part of the Act because, as mentioned, Congress recognized that the Guard had a legitimate need to employ a small number of nondual status technicians. Applying the mandatory retirement/prompt separation provisions contained in this part of the Act to non-dual-status technicians in the National Guard would run counter to Congress's intent of allowing the Guard to employ this type of technician as a permanent part of its technician workforce.

# SECTION 522: ITS IMPACT ON VARIOUS GROUPS OF MILITARY TECHNICIANS IN THE ARMY RESERVE AND THE AIR FORCE RESERVE

## Army and Air Force Reserve Technicians Hired on or Before February 10, 1996, Who Held Dual-status on October 5, 1999

Provided they maintain their dual-status, these technicians will not be affected by the changes contained in the National Defense Authorization Act for FY2000; however, should they lose their dual-status[19] at some point after October 5, 1999, they will be substantially affected. Those who lose their dual-status and are eligible for an "unreduced annuity"[20] will be required to retire within 30 days of losing dual-status. (It is important to point out that the annuity, or pension, referred to here is the annuity earned by technicians *as members of the civil service*. It does not refer to the military retired pay which some technicians become eligible for as long-time members of the Selected Reserve).[21] Those who lose their dual-status but are *not* eligible for an unreduced annuity will have several options. They will have the opportunity to "(i) reapply for, and if

---

[19] A technician could lose his or her dual status (i.e. membership in the Selected Reserve) in several ways, including the following: failure to meet military physical standards, failure to be selected for promotion to the next higher military rank within the prescribed period of time, or through disciplinary actions which lead to the technicians discharge from the reserves or ineligibility for re-enlistment. In the first two cases, the technician would generally be considered to have lost dual-status involuntarily, while in the latter case the technician would be considered to have lost dual-status voluntarily.

[20] "For purposes of this section, a technician shall be considered to be eligible for an unreduced annuity if the technician is eligible for an annuity under section 8336, 8412, or 8414 of title 5 that is not subject to a reduction by reason of the age or years of service of the technician." P. L. 106-65, section 522(a); October 5, 1999. Title 10, U.S. Code, Section 10218(c). Section 8336 of title 5 deals with immediate retirement under the Civil Service Retirement System; Section 8412 of title 5 deals with immediate retirement under the Federal Employees' Retirement System; Section 8414 of title 5 deals with early retirement under the Federal Employees' Retirement System. The practical implications of this definition of unreduced annuity on individual technicians are discussed later in the report.

[21] As members of the civil service, technicians can earn an entitlement to an annuity either under the Civil Service Retirement System (CSRS) or under the Federal Employee Retirement System (FERS). Generally, a federal employee must have 30 years of qualifying *civil service* and be 55 years of age in order to be entitled to an unreduced annuity, although this is not always the case. (See footnote 30 for more information on this topic). Technicians may also be eligible for military retired pay. To qualify for military retired pay, they normally must have 20 years of qualifying *military service*, the last eight of which must in the reserves, and be at least 60 years of age. Since the end of the Cold War, however, these requirements have been temporarily lowered to facilitate reserve force reductions.

qualified, be appointed to, a position as a military technician (dual status); or (ii) apply for a civil service position that is not a technician position."[22]

Alternatively, these technicians can continue their employment with the Army or Air Force Reserves as non-dual-status technicians; however, they will have several conditions attached to their employment. First, they will *not* be permitted to apply for voluntary personnel actions[23] after October 5, 2000. Second, they will be required to retire within 30 days of becoming eligible for an unreduced annuity.

## Army and Air Force Reserve Technicians Hired on or Before February 10, 1996, Who Did Not Hold Dual-status on October 5, 1999

If they are eligible for an unreduced annuity, these technicians will be required to retire no later than April 5, 2000. If they are *not* eligible for an unreduced annuity, they will have the opportunity to "(i) reapply for, and if qualified, be appointed to, a position as a military technician (dual-status); or (ii) apply for a civil service position that is not a technician position."[24] Alternatively, these technicians can continue their employment with the Army or Air Force Reserves as non-dual-status technicians; however, they will have several conditions attached to their employment. First, they will *not* be permitted to apply for voluntary personnel actions after October 5, 2000. Second, they will be required to retire within 30 days of becoming eligible for an unreduced annuity.

---

[22] P. L. 106-65, section 522(a); October 5, 1999. Title 10, U.S. Code, Section 10218 (a)(3)(A).
[23] In this section, the term 'voluntary personnel action,' with respect to a non-dual status technician, means any of the following: (1) The hiring, entry, appointment, reassignment, promotion, or transfer of the technician into a position for which the Secretary concerned has established a requirement that the person occupying the position be a military technician (dual status). (2) Promotion to a higher grade if the technician is in a position for which the Secretary concerned has established a requirement that the person occupying the position be a military technician (dual status)." P. L. 106-65, section 522 (a); October 5, 1999. Title 10, U.S. Code, Section 10218(d).
[24] P. L. 106-65, section 522(a); October 5, 1999. Title 10, U.S. Code, Section 10218 (b)(2)(A).

**Table 1.** Effect of P.L. 106-65, Section 522, on Military Technicians in the Army Reserve and Air Force Reserve

| Hired on or before February 10, 1996? | Held Dual Status on October 5, 1999? | Affected by P.L. 106-65, section 522? | Effect on Technician |
|---|---|---|---|
| Yes | No | Yes | If eligible for an unreduced annuity, the technician will be retired no later than April 5, 2000.<br><br>If not eligible for unreduced annuity, technician has three options:<br><br>(1) regain reserve membership and reapply for position;<br>(2) apply for a nontechnician position in the civil service;<br>(3) continue in their job as a non-dual-status technician. However, the technician will then be:<br>(a) ineligible for voluntary personnel actions after October 5, 2000, and:<br>(b) will be retired within 30 days of becoming eligible for an unreduced annuity. |
| Yes | Yes, and maintains it in the future | No | None |
| Yes | Yes, but loses it in the future | Yes | If eligible for an unreduced annuity when dual status is lost, the technician will be retired within 30 days.<br>If not eligible for unreduced annuity when dual status is lost, technician has three options:<br>(1) regain reserve membership and reapply for position;<br>(2) apply for a nontechnician position in the civil service.<br>(3) continue in their job as a non-dual status technician.<br>However, the technician will then be:<br>(a) ineligible for voluntary personnel actions after October 5, 2000, and;<br>(b) will be retired within 30 days of becoming eligible for an unreduced annuity. |

**Table 1.** Effect of P.L. 106-65, Section 522, on Military Technicians in the Army Reserve and Air Force Reserve (continued)

| Hired on or before February 10, 1996? | Held Dual Status on October 5, 1999? | Affected by P.L. 106-65, section 522? | Effect on Technician |
|---|---|---|---|
| No | No | Yes | If eligible for an unreduced annuity, the technician will be retired no later than April 5, 2000. If not eligible for unreduced annuity, technician has three options: (1) regain reserve membership and reapply for position; (2) apply for a nontechnician position in the civil service. (3) continue in their job as a non-dual status technician. However, the technician will then be: (a) ineligible for voluntary personnel actions after October 5, 2000, and; (b) will be separated from employment within one year of losing dual-status. |
| No | Yes, and maintains it in the future | No | None |
| No | Yes, but loses it in the future | Yes | If eligible for an unreduced annuity when dual status is lost, the technician will be retired within 30 days. If not eligible for unreduced annuity when dual status is lost, technician has three options: (1) regain reserve membership and reapply for position; (2) apply for a nontechnician position in the civil service. (3) continue in their job as a non-dual status technician. However, the technician will then be: (a) ineligible for voluntary personnel actions after October 5, 2000, and; (b) will be separated from employment within one year of losing dual status. |

## Army and Air Force Reserve Technicians Hired after February 10, 1996, Who Held Dual Status on October 5, 1999

Provided they maintain their dual-status, these technicians will not be affected by the changes contained in the National Defense Authorization Act for FY2000; however, should they lose their dual-status at some point after October 5, 1999, they will be substantially affected. If they lose their dual-status and are eligible for an unreduced annuity, they will be required to retire from their positions within 30 days of losing dual-status. Those who lose their dual-status but are *not* eligible for an unreduced annuity will have several options. They will have the opportunity to "(i) reapply for, and if qualified, be appointed to, a position as a military technician (dual status); or (ii) apply for a civil service position that is not a technician position."[25]

Alternatively, these technicians can continue their employment with the Army or Air Force Reserves as non-dual-status technicians; however, they will *not* be permitted to apply for any voluntary personnel actions after October 5, 2000, and they will be separated from their employment not later than one year after the date on which dual status was lost.

## Army and Air Force Reserve Technicians Hired after February 10, 1996, Who Did Not Hold Dual Status on October 5, 1999

If they are eligible for an unreduced annuity, these technicians will be required to retire no later than April 5, 2000. If they are *not* eligible for an unreduced annuity, they will have the opportunity to "(i) reapply for, and if qualified, be appointed to, a position as a military technician (dual-status); or (ii) apply for a civil service position that is not a technician position."[26] Alternatively, these technicians can continue their employment with the Army or Air Force Reserves as non-dual-status technicians; however, they will *not* be permitted to apply for any voluntary personnel actions after October 5, 2000, and they will be separated from their employment not later than one year after the date on which dual status was lost.

---

[25] P. L. 106-65, section 522(a); October 5, 1999. Title 10, U.S. Code, Section 10218 (a)(3)(A)
[26] P. L. 106-65, section 522(a); October 5, 1999. Title 10, U.S. Code, Section 10218 (b)(2)(A).

## IMPACT OF THE MANDATORY RETIREMENT PROVISIONS ON INDIVIDUAL TECHNICIANS

The mandatory retirement provisions mentioned above will cause an estimated 308 technicians, almost all of whom are employed by the Army Reserve, to be retired no later than April 5, 2000.[27] These are technicians who were hired on or before February 10, 1996, did not hold dual-status on October 5, 1999, and *were eligible* for an unreduced civil service annuity on the latter date. By the end of fiscal year 2005, it is estimated that an additional 779 technicians will be similarly forced to retire, with a further 358 retired by the end of fiscal year 2016. These are technicians who were hired on or before February 10, 1996, did not hold dual-status on October 5, 1999, but *were ineligible* for an unreduced annuity on the latter date. Pursuant to the law they will be retired within six months of becoming eligible for an unreduced annuity.

This projection, however, does not account for technicians who were hired on or before February 10, 1996, and held dual status on October 5, 1999, but who lose their dual status at some future date. According to the law, these technicians will also be required to retire when they become eligible for an unreduced annuity.

As mentioned above, those Army and Air Force Reserve technicians hired after February 10, 1996, will not be allowed to stay in their positions until retirement if they lose their dual-status. However, the legislation does allow them to stay in their positions for up to one year after losing dual-status. Thus, under this legislation, there likely will be a small number of non-dual-status technicians who are permitted to continue working during this one year transition period on an ongoing basis.

Consequently, the legislation permanently authorizes up to 175 non-dual-status technicians in both the Army and Air Force Reserves after October 1, 2007, in order to accommodate these technicians.

---

[27] Source: Colonel Richard Krimmer, Department of Defense, Office of the Assistant Secretary of Defense for Reserve Affairs. According to Colonel Krimmer, these figures are the best available at the present time, but they may fluctuate in the future. The interpretation of precisely who is eligible for an "unreduced annuity" will be a key factor in determining precisely how many technicians will be affected. (See footnote 30 for more information on this issue). Tom Hawley, Professional Staff Member, House Armed Services Committee, cites a figure of 387 technicians who will be retired by April 5, 2000.

## ARGUMENTS IN OPPOSITION TO THE
## MANDATORY RETIREMENT PROVISIONS

The mandatory retirement provision has been criticized by some, especially by those non-dual-status technicians who will soon be forced into retirement. Their principal criticism is that the legislation is unfair to them, as it forces them to retire and receive a pension check when they would prefer to continue working and receive a full paycheck. The difference between a civil service retirement payment and a regular paycheck is substantial, although it will vary from individual to individual, depending on each individual's total years of service. For example, assume a nondual-status technician plans to retire at age 60 after 35 years of service. At that time, the technician would be eligible for an annuity equal to 66.25% of his or her "high-3" average pay.[28] If, on the other hand, that same technician is required to retire at age 55 after 30 years of service, the difference between pay and pension will be greater.

This technician will immediately be eligible to receive a civil service pension check, but it will equal 56.25% of his or her "high-3" average pay. Thus, assuming the individual does not find alternate employment, between the age of 55 and 60, the technician's gross income will be reduced by 43.75% (full paycheck minus pension check), and after age 60 the technician's gross income will be 15% lower than anticipated (an annuity of 56.25% of pay is worth 15% less than an annuity of 66.25%).[29] Thus, assuming that they had a desire to continue working, the technicians who are retired under this provision could experience a significant reduction in income from the federal government. These retired technicians are free to seek employment in the private sector, and the combination of their private sector earnings with their civil service pension could result in their earning a higher income than before. However, as these technicians will all be at least 55 years of age at the time they retire, opponents of the mandatory retirement provisions argue that they may have a difficult time securing employment in the private sector.[30]

---

[28] The accrual rates for each year of service under CSRS are 1.5% for the first five years, 1.75% for the second five years, and 2.0% for all subsequent years. This factor is then applied to the average of the employees highest three years of pay to determine the annuity.

[29] Note, however, that the difference in net income will not be as great as the difference in gross income. A technician who is covered by CSRS has 7% of gross pay deducted from each paycheck in order to fund his or her pension. That deduction is not taken out of pension payments

[30] Most of the technicians who will be immediately affected by the mandatory retirement provisions were hired prior to January 1, 1984 and most of them are covered by the Civil Service Retirement System (CSRS). Thus, the example cited here is based on the parameters of CSRS. The age used here, 55 years, reflects the normal minimum retirement age of federal employees under CSRS and the

To remedy this situation, some propose repealing the mandatory retirement provisions altogether, allowing non-dual-status technicians to continue working indefinitely as long as they can fulfill the civilian functions of their job. Others propose modifying the mandatory retirement provision so that it will not apply until the technician reaches age 60, the age at which many of these technicians will be eligible to receive their military retirement check for their years of reserve duty.[31]

Opponents of the mandatory retirement provisions reject the notion that nondual-status technicians undermine the readiness of reserve units. They argue that such a relationship has never been conclusively demonstrated.[32] On the contrary, they argue that military technicians, whether dual-status or not, contribute substantially to the readiness of reserve units. From this perspective, requiring some of the most experienced technicians to retire will hurt the readiness of reserve units rather than enhancing it.

---

normal years of service, 30, needed to receive an unreduced annuity (Title 5, U.S. Code, section 8336 (a)). However, if involuntarily separated, federal employees covered by CSRS become eligible for an unreduced annuity at age 55 with 20 years of service or age 62 with five years of service (Title 5, U.S. Code, section 8336 (d); Title 5, U.S. Code, section 8336 (f); Title 5, U.S. Code, section 8339 (h)). Thus, under this retirement authority some technicians could be forced to retire at age 55 with 20 years of service, with an annuity worth 36.25% of their "high-3" pay. There has been some disagreement over whether Congress intended this involuntary separation retirement authority to apply to non-dual-status technicians. However, Ted Newland from the Retirement Policy Division of the Office of Personnel Management recently stated that he "met with staff of the House Armed Service and Government Reform committees, and provided technical assistance in drafting the bill. Not only are the above criteria [the retirement age/years of service combinations] consistent with the plain wording of the statute, they are consistent with the intentions expressed in those discussions." While most of the technicians who will be immediately affected by the mandatory retirement provisions are covered by CSRS, a small number are covered by the Federal Employees Retirement System (FERS) rules for retirement, due to retirement system conversions or as a result of federal civil service credit for past military service. Under FERS, employees are eligible for an unreduced annuity at age 50 with 20 years of service, at age 62 with five years of service, or at any age with 25 years of service. (Title 5, U.S. Code, section 8414 (b)). The accrual rates under FERS are 1% per year of service. The resultant factor is then applied to the employees "high-3" pay to determine the value of the annuity.

[31] As pointed out in footnote 21, technicians can qualify for two distinct types of retirement pay: a civil service pension and military retired pay. Note, however, that technicians do not automatically qualify for military retired pay. To be eligible, a technician must have completed at least twenty qualifying years of military service, either on active duty or as a member of the Selected Reserve. Precisely because non-dual-status technicians lost their membership in the Selected Reserve at some point in their career, there is good reason to believe that some of them are not eligible for military retired pay.

[32] John Esposito, President, Local 1900, American Federation of Government Employees.

## Arguments in Support of the Mandatory Retirement Provisions

Supporters of the mandatory retirement provisions reject the notion that mandatory retirement will undermine readiness; in fact, their principal argument is that it will enhance the readiness of the reserve units, especially those within the Army Reserve (which has the highest proportion of non-dual status technicians). Non-dual status technicians, they argue, may do excellent work in their civilian capacity, but they cannot fulfill all the duties of their jobs unless they can be mobilized and deployed with their units. This inability to deploy creates a situation where some of the key, full-time personnel of a unit (the non-dual-status technicians) will remain at their home-station while the less experienced, part-time personnel (traditional reservists) deploy to the theater of operations. This, they argue, deprives the unit of key personnel precisely when they are needed most and thereby degrades the efficiency and effectiveness of the unit. The way to remedy it is to replace non-dual-status technicians with dual-status technicians, who will be able to deploy with their units in the event of a mobilization.

While conceding that non-dual-status technicians might not like the mandatory retirement provisions, supporters of the provisions argue that the provisions are fair. Recognizing that there was no clear dual status policy prior to February 10, 1996, the provisions allow the Department of Defense to continue employing technicians who were hired before that date until they are eligible for an unreduced civil service pension, regardless of whether or not they hold dual-status. Allowing these technicians to continue working until eligible for an unreduced pension, it is argued, is a fair way to reconcile the legitimate needs of the military with the legitimate career expectations of the technicians; and in any case, it is a solution that is far preferable to the reductions-in-force that would have occurred under the original plan to eliminate all non-dual-status technicians by 2007.

## Other Considerations

The debate over the mandatory retirement provisions has generally been framed within the context of whether or not they strike an appropriate balance between military readiness and fairness to technicians. Supporters of the provisions say that they do strike the proper balance. Opponents say that they do not. However, another perspective deserves mention; namely, some may question whether the mandatory retirement provisions are unduly generous to technicians and, as a result, undermine the readiness of reserve units. If one accepts the argument that employment of nondual-status technicians in the technician workforce works to the detriment of the readiness of reserve units, then there are aspects of the mandatory retirement provisions which may be troubling from a military readiness perspective.

Specifically, the existing provisions allow for the continued employment of any military technicians in the Army and Air Force Reserve who have lost their dualstatus, or who lose it in the future, provided they were hired on or before February 10, 1996. At present, 72% of all Army Reserve technicians and 99% of all Air Force Reserve technicians were hired on or before February 10, 1996.[33] Thus, a large number of technicians are potentially eligible to continue employment in their positions as non-dual-status technicians. While there are substantial drawbacks associated with this position status – such as ineligibility for promotion or transfer – they may be tolerable, especially for technicians who are happy in the position they currently occupy, who have already reached the top of their promotion ladder, or who are less employable in the private sector. In light of this, it is conceivable that a significant number of technicians will choose to drop their reserve membership, or will fail to maintain the standards necessary to maintain reserve membership, with the understanding that they will be "protected" from separation until they are eligible for retirement. Such a phenomenon could be particularly acute in the Air Force Reserve, which has historically imposed a fairly strict dual-status requirement on its technicians and which might see that policy undercut by a provision which appears to guarantee a full career to all technicians hired before February 10, 1996, whether they hold dualstatus or not.[34]

When considering this possibility, it is important to note that the legislation does not *require* the Department of Defense to allow non-dual-status technicians to continue in their technician positions until they qualify for retirement; the legislation only *permits* this to happen, by allowing DoD to employ these technicians until 30 days after they become retirement-eligible. However, given

---

[33] Source: Colonel Richard Krimmer, Department of Defense, Office of the Assistant Secretary of Defense for Reserve Affairs.

[34] A rise in the proportion of non-dual-status technicians within the Air Force Reserve would be particularly troubling from the perspective of readiness given that the Air Force Reserve routinely uses its technicians to fill critical positions like air commander, base commander, pilot, and navigator. According to Colonel Richard Krimmer (Department of Defense, Office of the Assistant Secretary of Defense for Reserve Affairs), the Air Force is unlikely to use the authority granted by Congress to keep non-dual-status technicians in their positions until eligible for retirement. Rather, it will almost certainly continue to enforce its dual-status requirement and separate those technicians who lose their reserve membership. This could trigger complaints of unfairness, however.

that the legislation was written in response to concerns raised by DoD about fairness to the career expectations of technicians, it seems likely that the Department will use this continuation authority liberally. To do otherwise would allow certain non-dual-status technicians to continue on until retirement, while forcing others out without that benefit. This would inevitably reopen the whole issue of "fairness" that DoD was so concerned about in its 1999 report to Congress.[35]

## THE ONGOING DEBATE

Although Congress established a clear policy in 1999 when it enacted the mandatory retirement provisions for non-dual-status technicians in the Army and Air Force Reserve, some technicians and their advocates are currently lobbying to have that policy repealed or modified. A repeal of the mandatory retirement provisions would return the situation to the *status quo ante*: Non-dual-status technicians hired before February 10, 1996 (when the dual-status requirement was fixed in law) would be allowed to continue their careers in the same manner as dual status technicians, retiring only when they chose to do so. Under such a policy, non-dual-status technicians would be phased out of the technician workforce much more slowly than they will be under the current mandatory retirement provisions.

Another proposal currently being advanced by some is to modify the mandatory retirement provisions so that non-dual-status technicians will not be forced to retire before the age of 60. If enacted, such a change would allow the affected technicians to continue working for up to five years longer, extending the period in which they earn a full paycheck and increasing the size of their retirement annuity. Additionally, at age 60, many technicians become eligible for the military retired pay they have earned as members of the Selected Reserve. Thus, under this proposal, the difference in income between regular pay and retirement pay would be decreased for most affected technicians. However, if such a policy change were enacted, non-dual-status technicians would be phased out of the technician workforce more slowly than they will be under the current mandatory retirement provisions (but more quickly than they would be if the mandatory retirement provisions were repealed).

---

[35] Department of Defense, Office of the Assistant Secretary of Defense for Reserve Affairs, "A Plan for Full Utilization of Military Technicians (Dual Status)," August 2, 1999.

This latter proposal appears to be gaining support in Congress. On March 2, 2000, the chairman and ranking member of the Military Personnel subcommittee of the House Armed Service Committee sent a letter to the Secretary of Defense stating that "we have become aware of the need to revise certain portions of section 10218 [of Title 10 U.S.C.] to permit the mandatory separation to take place at age 60, instead of age 55. We are working to make this change part of the National Defense Authorization Act for Fiscal Year 2001." The letter also indicated that the authors supported a proposal advanced by the Army to temporarily rehire those technicians who will be separated on April 5, 2000, pending congressional consideration of the revised retirement age in the National Defense Authorization Act for FY2001.

# APPENDIX A
# ORIGIN AND EVOLUTION OF THE MILITARY TECHNICIAN PROGRAM AND THE DUAL STATUS REQUIREMENT

Military technicians are descended from the personnel described in Section 90 of the National Defense Act of 1916.[36] This act, which dramatically reshaped the relationship between the state militias and the federal Army, authorized the use of federal funds "for the compensation of competent help" to take care of the "material, animals, and equipment" in those organized militia units known as the National Guard.[37] In subsequent legislation, the phrase "competent help" was replaced with "caretakers and clerks."

From the program's inception in 1916, the personnel employed under this legislative authority remained state employees, although they were paid with federal funds. However, this changed in 1968 when Congress passed the National Guard Technicians Act.[38] This act converted all of the National Guard's "caretakers and clerks" from state employees paid with federal funds to federal employees subject to a certain measure of state control and administration. It also renamed them "technicians."

For many years, the military technician program existed only within the National Guard. However, in the late 1950s, both the Air Force Reserve and the

---

[36] Statutes at Large, June 13, 1916, chapter 134, section 90.
[37] According to the National Defense Act of 1916 the militia of the United States was composed of all able-bodied male citizens between the ages of 18 and 45. The militia was then subdivided into three groups: the Unorganized Militia, the Naval Militia, and the National Guard. Statutes at Large, June 13, 1916, chapter 134, sections 57.
[38] P. L. 90-486; 82 Stat. 755; August 13, 1968.

Army Reserve decided to establish their own military technician programs.[39] Unlike the National Guard program, which was established by independent statutory provisions, the Reserve programs were established administratively, under the broader statutory umbrella of the federal civil service. The Air Force Reserve formally established its technician program in 1957 by successfully negotiating an agreement with the Civil Service Commission (later the Office of Personnel Management). The Army Reserve also wanted to establish a technician program in the late 1950s, but the Civil Service Commission decided to postpone approval for such a program until it had a chance to assess the Air Force Reserve's program. The Air Force Reserve's technician program was a novel modification of traditional civil service rules and the Civil Service Commission was reluctant to expand the program until its impact on federal employees (the technicians) could be assessed.

In 1960, the Civil Service Commission rendered a fairly negative assessment of the Air Force Reserve's technician program. In the eyes of the Commission, the program was plagued by problems that resulted from its unique mix of civilian and military functions. In a letter to the Assistant Secretary of Defense, the chairman of the Civil Service Commission stated:

> A perfectly trouble-free operation for the undertaking of the magnitude and novelty of the Air Reserve Technician [ART] program had not been anticipated. However, the difficulties that have been encountered have been sufficiently serious to cause misgivings about the wisdom of entering upon another similar program...There have been complaints about inappropriate imposition of military discipline on civilians in such matters as standing at attention, saluting, and wearing uniforms. Nonreservists have complained that their jobs have been abolished only to reappear with an ART incumbent. We have had allegations that civilians who joined the Air Reserve to qualify for a technician job were later refused the job but not released from the Reserves. The failure to indoctrinate appointing officials with the true nature of the program and their responsibilities to it is indicated when an officer informed one of our regional directors that he would disregard Civil Service rules and the Air Force agreement whenever it suited his purposes to do so.[40]

Despite these problems, the Civil Service Commission agreed to approve an Army Reserve technician program in 1960; however, the Commission insisted that the program be designed in such a way as to minimize or eliminate the type of

---

[39] There has never been a military technician program within the Naval Reserve, Marine Corps Reserve, or the Coast Guard Reserve.

[40] Letter from Roger W. Jones, Chairman of the Civil Service Commission, to Charles C. Finucane, Assistant Secretary of Defense, February 23, 1960.

problems associated with the Air Force Reserve program. The Memorandum of Understanding (MOU) reached between the Civil Service Commission and the Department of the Army was drafted with this goal in mind.[41] As such, the agreement which governed the Army Reserve's technician program at its inception differed substantially from that of the Air Force Reserve. Furthermore, in certain respects, the provisions of both Reserve technician programs differed from those of the National Guard. One of the key areas of difference among the three military technician programs – National Guard, Air Force Reserve, and Army Reserve – was in the stringency of the dual status requirement for the military technicians employed. The different "dual status" provisions in the National Guard, Air Force Reserve, and Army Reserve are outlined below.

## "DUAL STATUS" PROVISIONS IN THE NATIONAL GUARD'S TECHNICIAN PROGRAM

The National Guard's "dual status" provisions can be traced back to the National Defense Act of 1916. While providing the National Guard with federal funds to hire "competent help," the act also required that the "the men to be compensated, not to exceed five for each battery or troop, shall be duly enlisted therein."[42] However, exceptions to this general policy were made soon thereafter. In 1924, for example, Congress amended the National Defense Act of 1916 to authorize the use of civilian employees "whenever it shall be found impracticable to secure the necessary competent enlisted caretakers...."[43] Similarly broad exceptions were contained in later versions of the statute. Despite these broad exceptions, the National Guard managed the technician program in such a way that its technician workforce was almost exclusively dual status. In 1968, Congress estimated that 95% of National Guard technicians held dual status.[44] In that same year, Congress passed the National Guard Technicians Act[45] which converted National Guard technicians from state to federal employees. The act

---

[41] Memorandum of Understanding dated July 5, 1960.
[42] Statutes at Large, June 3, 1916, chapter 134, section 90. "Batteries," "Troops," and "Companies" are Army units generally commanded by a captain or first lieutenant and having anywhere from 60 to 180 soldiers, depending on the type of unit.
[43] Statutes at Large, June 6, 1924, P. L. 207, Chapter 275, section 5.
[44] "About 95% of the technicians are required to hold concurrent National Guard membership as a condition for their civilian employment." House Report No. 1823, Conference Report to Accompany S. 3865, the National Guard Technicians Act of 1968. U.S. Code Congressional and Administrative News, Legislative History for P. L. 90-486, 3319.
[45] P. L. 90-486; 82 Stat. 755; August 13, 1968.

also stipulated that every technician working for the National Guard would simultaneously "be a member of the National Guard," except as specifically prescribed by the Secretary of the Army or Air Force.[46] (In 1997, the language allowing the service Secretaries to make exceptions to the dual status requirement was deleted).[47] As a result of this fairly strict dual status requirement, the National Guard's technician workforce has remained overwhelmingly dual status. Since 1968, dual status technicians have constituted about 90 to 95% of the total technician workforce in the National Guard.[48] The Department of Defense recently reported that 95% of National Guard technicians held dual status at the end of fiscal year 1998. This figure represents the average of the figures for Army National Guard technicians (91% of whom hold dual status) and Air National Guard technicians (99% of whom hold dual-status).[49]

## "DUAL STATUS" PROVISIONS IN THE AIR FORCE RESERVE'S TECHNICIAN PROGRAM

The Memorandum of Agreement (MOA) reached by the Air Force Reserve and the Civil Service Commission in 1957 contained a fairly strict "dual status" requirement. It stipulated that "For all ART [Air Reserve Technician] positions there will be an established requirement that persons appointed to these positions must be eligible for and willing to accept active membership in the reserve unit in which they would be employed."[50] It further stated that "Employees who develop physical disabilities or conditions which do not permit continued reserve membership may not continue indefinitely in the ART category."[51] Subsequent

---

[46] P. L. 90-486; 82 Stat. 755, Section 709 (b); August 13, 1968. Congress did, however, anticipate that the National Guard would have need for a small number of technicians who did not hold dual status in the 1968 National Guard Technicians Act. The report language accompanying the bill noted that, under the new law, "about 95% of the technicians would hold noncompetitive positions and would be required to be members of the Guard as a part of their civilian employment. About 5%, or 2,000, would be in a competitive federal status and would constitute principally female employees, clerk-typists, and security guards." House Report No. 1823, Conference Report to Accompany S. 3865, the National Guard Technicians Act of 1968. U.S. Code Congressional and Administrative News, Legislative History for P. L. 90-486, 3324.
[47] P. L. 105-85, section 522 (c); 111 Stat. 1735; November 18, 1997.
[48] Department of Defense, Office of the Assistant Secretary of Defense for Reserve Affairs, "A Plan for Full Utilization of Military Technicians (Dual Status)," August 2, 1999, page 2.
[49] Department of Defense, Office of the Assistant Secretary of Defense for Reserve Affairs, "A Plan for Full Utilization of Military Technicians (Dual Status)," August 2, 1999, page 2.
[50] John W. Macy, Jr., Executive Director, United States Civil Service Commission, Commission Letter No. 57-45, "The Air Reserve Technician Plan for Air Reserve Flying Centers Within The Continental Air Command," June 28, 1957, 4.
[51] John W. Macy, Jr., Commission Letter No. 57-45, June 28, 1957, 5.

versions of this agreement have included a similarly strong dual status requirement.[52] Depending on the importance of the position they occupied, technicians who lost their dual status were either subject to separation from their technician position, or allowed to continue in their technician position only until they could be placed in a non-technician position of similar or higher grade.

As a result of this fairly strict "dual status" requirement, the Air Force Reserve's technician workforce has been almost entirely dual status. The Air Force Reserve has allowed some technicians to continue working in their civilian capacity if they lost their dual status through no fault of their own, yet the number of technicians treated in this way is quite small. In fiscal year 1998, only one percent of the technicians in the Air Force Reserve could be described as "non-dual-status."[53]

## "DUAL STATUS" PROVISIONS IN THE ARMY RESERVE'S TECHNICIAN PROGRAM

In contrast to the fairly strict "dual status" requirement contained in the agreement governing the Air Force Reserve's program, the 1960 Memorandum of Understanding (MOU) governing the Army Reserve's program had a more flexible provision. For example, while the Air Force Reserve program required technicians to be members of the Air Force Reserve when hired, this was not an absolute requirement in the Army Reserve program. According to the Army's MOU, certain circumstances – such as a tight labor market – might make the use of dual status technicians impractical. In such cases, "any available qualified civilians, including women, will be employed through usual civil service procedures."[54] Thus, "under this program, individuals who were eligible for membership in the Army Reserve were the primary recruitment source for military technicians. Individuals not eligible for Reserve membership constituted

---

[52] "Recruitment of Air Reserve Technicians Through Competitive Agreement (ART Agreement)," United States Office of Personnel Management, basic document approved 24 January 1979; republished with authorized changes 1 December 1987.
[53] In fiscal year 1998, there were 113 technicians in the Air Force Reserve who did not hold dual status, out of a total technician population of 9,263. The Air Force Reserve prefers to refer to these technicians as "status quo" rather than as "non-dual-status" in order to highlight the fact that all of its technicians were required to hold dual-status when hired; none was hired as a "non-dual-status" technician. Yet, the fact remains that these "status quo" technicians do not now hold dual status. Thus, they can accurately be referred to as "non-dual-status" technicians, as the term is used in this report.
[54] Memorandum of Understanding, dated July 5, 1960, paragraph 1.

a secondary recruitment source when Reservists were not available."[55] Another difference between the Army and Air Force Reserve programs was the way in which the programs treated technicians who lost their military membership. Under the Air Force rules, technicians who lost their military status, for any reason, were normally separated from the program. Under the Army rules, technicians who lost their military status voluntarily could be separated from the program, although this was not mandated. More importantly, technicians who lost their military status involuntarily – for example, by sustaining an injury that precluded meeting the physical standards of the military – could *not* be separated from the program.[56]

In 1970, the Army Reserve re-negotiated its MOU with the Civil Service Commission and incorporated a somewhat stricter dual-status requirement.[57] The new agreement stated that "membership in an active Army Reserve Unit (or eligibility and willingness to join the Reserve) shall be a requirement to secure a permanent appointment to a position as a technician...." There were still some exceptions to this policy, but it was certainly a stronger "dual status" provision than had previously been the case. This provision, however, only applied to the technician at the time of initial appointment; it did not constitute an ongoing requirement to maintain military membership. Indeed, the MOU specifically states that "No technician who attains dual status and later loses his active reserve status for reasons outside his control will be involuntarily reassigned or removed."[58] The MOU also contained an explicit "grandfather" clause to protect those technicians who had been hired under the terms of the previous MOU and who did not hold dual-status.[59] Thus, while the 1970 MOU strengthened the "dual-status" provisions in the Army Reserve's technician program with respect to initial hiring for technician positions, it still left ample room for the continued employment of non-dual status technicians.

---

[55] Military Technician Compensation Report: A Report Prepared for the House Appropriations Committee, Office of the Secretary of Defense (Reserve Affairs), May, 1991, 4.

[56] Memorandum of Understanding, dated July 5, 1960, paragraph 2. "The lack or involuntary loss of military status will not be a basis for removing present or future civilian employees."

[57] The effective date of the new Memorandum of Understanding was September 1, 1970.

[58] Army Regulation 140-315, Employment and Utilization of U.S. Army Reserve Military Technicians, 5 July 1985, Appendix A, Memorandum of Understanding, paragraph 7.

[59] "No technician employed prior to 1 September 1970 who is not in a dual civilian military status on that date will be involuntarily reassigned or removed from his position for failure to comply with the dual status requirement." Army Regulation 140-315, Employment and Utilization of U.S. Army Reserve Military Technicians, 5 July 1985, Appendix A, Memorandum of Understanding, paragraph 7.

## APPENDIX B: CONGRESS AND THE DUAL STATUS REQUIREMENT: PAST LEGISLATIVE PROVISIONS

Over the past 16 years, Congress has repeatedly passed legislation concerning the dual status requirement for military technicians. Often, this legislation has been directed exclusively towards technicians in the Army Reserve, reflecting a special congressional concern with the manner in which the Army Reserve was managing its technician workforce. In recent years, however, Congress's approach to the issue has been more general in scope, although the Army Reserve's technician program has remained the principal concern.

When Congress passed the National Guard Technicians Act in 1968,[60] it contained a fairly strict dual status requirement for National Guard military technicians. However, this act did not apply to the Army Reserve or the Air Force Reserve. These two reserve branches had set their own dual status policies for many years and Congress took no action to change that in 1968. This changed, however, in 1983. Concerned about the growing proportion of non-dual-status technicians in the Army Reserve, Congress included a provision in the Department of Defense Appropriation Act for Fiscal Year 1984 which addressed the dual status requirement for Army Reserve technicians. The report which accompanied the bill in the House criticized the proportion of non-dual-status technicians – referred to as "status quo" technicians – within the Army Reserve in the following terms:

> The Department of the Army estimates that approximately 50% of the United States Army Reserve [technicians] are either status quo technicians or military technicians assigned to units other than the one in which they are employed as a civilian. The Committee believes this situation is detrimental to mobilization readiness and unit cohesiveness.[61]

To correct this, the final version of the defense appropriation bill included language which prohibited the expenditure of funds to pay for any Army Reserve technician "initially hired after the date of enactment of the act...unless such individual is also a military member of the Army Reserve troop program unit that

---

[60] P. L. 90-486, 82 Stat. 755; August 13, 1968.
[61] House Report Number 98-427. Report to Accompany H.R. 4185, Department of Defense Appropriation Bill, 1984, 37. The ratio of technicians who were "status quo" versus those who were misassigned was not indicated in the House Report, but the General Accounting Office ascertained four years earlier that 26% of the dual-status technicians in the Army Reserve were assigned to military positions in units other than the one in which they are employed and an additional 20% of technicians were "status quo," or non-dual-status, technicians. H. L. Krieger, Director, General Accounting Office, Letter to Harold Brown, February 26, 1979.

he or she is employed to support."[62] Virtually identical language was included in every subsequent DoD Appropriations Act up to, and including, the DoD Appropriations Act for Fiscal Year 1995.[63]

On its face, this recurring provision would seem to preclude paying the salary of any technician whose initial date of hiring occurred after December 8, 1983 – the enactment date of the DoD Appropriations Act for FY1984 – and who did not hold or who failed to maintain "dual status." Indeed, the Army Reserve interpreted the appropriations language in just this way for many years. Nonetheless, due to lack of coordination within the Army Reserve's military technician program, this requirement was not always implemented; in some cases the employment contracts of technicians hired after December 8, 1983, did not include a clause specifying the technicians obligation to hold dual-status.[64] More problematically, in 1995 the Army Reserve substantially modified its interpretation of the appropriations language. This revised interpretation was spelled out in a 1995 memorandum:

> We have reexamined the status of the involuntary removal policies as they affect dual status MT [military technician] personnel. We have concluded, based on the current legal interpretations, the rules of post Fiscal Year 1983 (FY1983) dual status alignments only apply to the initial FY of MT employment. Subsequent to the initial year of employment, the MT dual status requirement revert to the conditions in force for MT[s] hired between FY1970 and FY1983. Therefore, we conclude MTs, not in their initial FY of employment, may be involuntarily separated from their Selected Reserve troop program unit without concurrent loss of MT civilian employment.[65]

As a result of this interpretation, the impact of the appropriations language on the Army Reserve's technician workforce was minimized. Newly hired

---

[62] P. L. 98-212, section 783; December 8, 1983. Note, however, that there was an exception to the unit membership requirement for those technicians "employed by the Army Reserve in areas other than Army Reserve troop program units." These technicians only needed to be "members of the Selected Reserve."

[63] P. L. 98-212, section 783; P. L. 98-473, section 8076; P. L. 99-190, section 8059; P. L. 99-591, section 9054; P. L. 100-202, section 8055; P. L. 100-463, section 8045; P. L. 101- 165, section 9027; P. L. 101-511, section 8018; P. L. 102-172, section 8018; P. L. 102-396, section 9019; P. L. 103-139, section 8016; and P. L. 103-335, section 8015.

[64] Source: Colonel Richard Krimmer, Department of Defense, Office of the Assistant Secretary of Defense for Reserve Affairs.

[65] "Memorandum for Commanders, Major U.S. Army Reserve Commands," from Colonel Thomas McCoy, Deputy Chief of Staff for Personnel, Headquarters, United States Army Reserve Command, 27 July 1995. The "current legal interpretations" referred to in the text apparently refers to a legal opinion issued by the Department of the Army's Judge Advocate General in February, 1995. A summary of this opinion was provided to the Congressional Research Service by the Office of the Judge Advocate General; however, that office declined to provide a copy of the opinion itself, citing attorney-client privilege. Thus, an analysis of its contents cannot be provided here.

technicians were now only required to hold dual-status until the end of the fiscal year in which they were hired; at the end of that fiscal year they fell under the provisions of the 1970 MOU, which allowed technicians who lost their military membership involuntarily to retain their civilian jobs. Moreover, all the technicians hired since December 8, 1983, now fell under this new policy as well. They too could lose their dual status and retain their civilian job, provided that their loss of dual-status was not a voluntary act.[66]

> Congress moved quickly to close this loophole. The funding ban provision in the DoD Appropriations Act for Fiscal Year 1996 was nearly identical to those passed in previous years, but an extra clause was added to the provision which extended the ban indefinitely.[67] By doing so, the legal justification for interpreting the appropriations language as a "one year only" dual-status requirement was eliminated. Nonetheless, this correction was not retroactive; it only applied to technicians hired in fiscal year 1996 or later. Thus, those Army Reserve technicians who were hired between FY1984 and FY1995 were no longer bound by a strict dual-status requirement. Rather, they were only bound by the less stringent dual-status requirement found in the 1970 MOU.

Several months later, Congress reinforced the appropriations language with a similar provision in the National Defense Authorization Act for Fiscal Year 1996:

> The Secretary of Defense shall require the Secretary of the Army and the Secretary of the Air Force to establish as a condition of employment for each individual who is hired after the date of the enactment of this section [February 10, 1996] as a military technician that the individual maintain membership in the Selected Reserve (so as to be a so-called 'dual-status' technician)...No Department of Defense funds may be spent for compensation for any military technician hired after the date of enactment of this section who is not a member of the Selected Reserve....[68]

---

[66] See footnote 19 for the distinction between voluntary and involuntary loss of dual-status.
[67] P. L. 104-61, section 8016. The new provision read "None of the funds appropriated for the Department of Defense *during the current fiscal year and hereafter* shall be obligated for the pay of any individual who is initially employed after the date of enactment of this Act as a technician...unless such individual is a member of the Army Reserve troop program unit that he or she is employed to support. Those technicians employed by the Army Reserve in areas other than Army Reserve troop program units need only be members of the Selected Reserve." (Italicized text indicates the major change from previous language).
[68] P. L. 104-106, section 513(c); 110 Stat. 306. The law made a small exception to this general rule for technicians whose "loss of membership in the Selected Reserve...was not due to the failure to meet military standards." These non-dual-status technicians could continue to receive compensation "for up to six months."

Although this language closely resembled that found in the earlier DoD Appropriations Act, it was broader in scope for it applied not only to the Army Reserve, but to the National Guard and Air Force Reserve as well.

In spite of these legislative provisions, the number of non-dual-status technicians in the Army Reserve continued to grow. In June of 1996, there were 785 non-dual status technicians in the Army Reserve; fifteen months later that number had doubled to 1,582.[69] In large part this phenomenon was attributable to a demographic imbalance within the Army Reserve's technician workforce. Many of the technicians had been hired in the 1960s and 1970s and, as they grew older, more and more were unable to maintain their military status due to physical or other reasons.[70] Realizing that its previous legislative actions were not having their intended effect, Congress returned to the issue in 1997.[71]

The National Defense Authorization Act for Fiscal Year 1998 contained several provisions related to military technicians and the "dual status" requirement. Specifically, it placed a limit on the number of non-dual-status technicians that could be employed in each of the technician programs – capping the number in the Army Reserve at 1,500 by the end of the fiscal year – and required the Secretary of Defense to submit a report to Congress outlining "a plan for ensuring that, on and after September 30, 2007, all military technician

---

[69] Source: Colonel Richard Krimmer, Department of Defense, Office of the Assistant Secretary of Defense for Reserve Affairs.

[70] The way in which the military promotion system operates is especially relevant here. The military promotion system has an "up or out" structure. Failure to be promoted to the next higher level within a specified time period can result in separation from the military. Moreover, as one advances through the ranks, chances for promotion decrease as there are fewer authorized positions for the higher ranks. Thus, after twenty or more years of service, a military technician might very well be passed over for military promotion – and later separated from the Selected Reserve – despite a generally strong performance record.

[71] The House National Security Committee explained its rationale for the military technician provisions contained in the National Defense Authorization Act for Fiscal Year 1998 in the following terms: "...the National Defense Authorization Act for Fiscal Year 1996 (Public Law 104-106) ...established hiring restrictions that were designed, in part, to reduce the numbers of military technicians who never were members of the selected reserve, or for one reason or another after being hired subsequently became disqualified from selected reserve membership...[T]he committee is disturbed to learn that contrary to the reductions in non-dual status technicians contemplated by the National Defense Authorization Act for Fiscal Year 1996....the number of non-dual status technicians in the Army Reserve has grown from almost 800 in fiscal year 1996 to nearly 1,300 in fiscal year 1997." House Report 105-132, Report to Accompany H. R. 1119, the National Defense Authorization Act for Fiscal Year 1998, 359. The figure cited in the report of "1,300 in fiscal year 1997" is significantly lower than the figure cited above of 1,582. The discrepancy can be attributed to fact that the former number comes from a House report issued on June 16, 1997, and reflects the figures available at that time, while the latter number reflects the situation on September 30, 1997.

positions are held only by military technicians (dual status)."[72] The clear implication of this latter provision was that Congress was seriously considering the abolition of all non-dual-status technicians and wanted advice from the Department of Defense on how to accomplish this objective.

The Department of Defense did submit a report to Congress in 1999 which contained a plan to ensure that only dual-status technicians held military technician positions by the end of FY2007; however, the report also raised a number of concerns about the fairness and feasibility of doing so. With respect to fairness, the report predicted that meeting the 2007 deadline would require DoD to involuntarily separate 2,655 non-dual-status technicians, many of whom would not be eligible for civil service retirement when separated.[73] Forced reductions of this sort, the DoD report argued, were unfair to the individual technicians:

> ...non-dual status military technicians were hired and are managed according to various Reserve component policies. Non-dual status military technicians had a reasonable expectation that their positions carried career potential. The Department feels a moral obligation to recognize previous commitments and reasonable individual career expectations and to avoid forced reductions to the extent practicable.

Another significant point raised in the DoD report dealt with the limited need for non-dual-status technicians in the National Guard. National Guard units usually operate under the authority of the Governor of the state or territory they are located in. Each state or territory maintains a headquarters to oversee its units and military technicians frequently are employed in these headquarters. If these technicians are dual-status, then they could be mobilized by the federal government in times of national emergency and deployed with the unit they maintain membership in. This, DoD contended, could cripple the ability of the state headquarters to carry out its own important mission. "The National Guard," the report concluded, "cannot operate without a workforce that includes some employees who do not have to mobilize with the units they support." From this perspective, the National Guard has an ongoing need for at least some non-dual-status technicians.

---

[72] P. L. 105-85, section 523; 111 Stat. 1737; November 18, 1997. The law also placed caps on the number of non-dual-status technicians which could be employed by the other Reserve organizations: No more that 450 non-dual-status technicians in the Air National Guard, 2,400 in the Army National Guard, and zero in the Air Force Reserve by the end of fiscal year 1998.

[73] Department of Defense, Office of the Assistant Secretary of Defense for Reserve Affairs, "A Plan for Full Utilization of Military Technicians (Dual Status)," August 2, 1999, pages 7 and 8. Numbers are derived from the estimated Reductions in Force (RIFs) required by September 30, 2007, without benefit of additional retirement incentives.

# INDEX

## A

accrual accounting, 64, 73, 74
across-the-board increases, 2, 5-7
active duty, 3-5, 8, 10, 14, 18, 20, 24, 26, 27, 37-45, 47, 53, 54, 58, 64, 66, 67, 69, 70, 73, 77, 78, 80, 81, 86, 99
active duty dependents, 24, 44, 45
Afghanistan, 20, 21
age, 3, 16, 17, 19, 20, 24-26, 32, 33, 35, 39-42, 44, 46-51, 55, 56, 63, 66-70, 72, 92, 98, 99, 102, 103
Air Force Reserve, 85, 86, 88, 89, 91-97, 101-107, 109, 112, 113
Air Force Reserve technicians, 101
Armed Forces Tax Fairness Act of 2003, 21
Army, 16, 22, 23, 27, 29, 39, 40, 48, 85, 86, 88-97, 100-113
Army Reserve, 86, 88-90, 101, 104, 105, 107-112
Army Reserve technicians, 109, 111

## B

Base Realignment and Closure, BRAC, 54
Basic allowance for housing, BAH, 7, 9
BAH housing costs, 10
Basic allowance for subsistence, BAS, 7, 9
BAS computations, 10
Bush Administration, 41, 63, 76

## C

career personnel, 3, 19, 68
career retention, 4
Centers for Medicare and Medicaid Services, 50
Civil Service Commission, 88, 104, 106, 108
civil service pension, 98-100
Civilian Health and Medical Program of the Uniformed Services, CHAMPUS, 25, 26, 37-44, 46, 51, 54, 55
civilian pay, 2, 8, 9, 14-18
civilian sector, 7, 46
Clinton, 50
Coalition of Retired Military Veterans, 28, 29
Cold War, 1, 4, 18, 42, 54, 75, 92
Combat Related Special Compensation, CRSC, 62, 78, 82
concurrent receipt, 61-63, 75-83
Congressional Budget Office, 22, 39, 52, 82
Constitution, 25
Consumer Price Index, 16, 57, 71
cost-of-living-adjustment, COLA, 16, 59, 67, 71, 72

## D

Defense Authorization Act of FY1996, 45
Defense Health Program, 40, 56
Defense Transformation for the 21st Century Act, 62, 69
Department of Defense, DOD, 2-4, 18, 22-24, 28, 32, 33, 37, 39-55, 58, 61, 62, 64,

65, 69, 70, 73, 75-80, 82, 75, 86, 89, 90, 97, 100-102, 106, 109-113
Department of Veterans' Affairs, 46
disabled retirees, 42, 76-78
draft, 3, 17, 51
dual status, 85-90, 92-97, 100, 102, 105-113

## E

educational levels, 16
Employment Cost Index, ECI, 8, 10-12, 14, 16
enrollment fees, 41, 48, 52

## F

Federal Employees Health Benefits Program, FEHBP, 31, 33, 34, 38, 48, 49, 52, 53, 56
free health care, 26, 27, 30
free lifetime care, 30, 31
FY1999 Defense Authorization Act, 48, 49, 53
FY2001 Defense Authorization Act, 38, 46, 48, 52, 55
FY2003 National Defense Authorization Act, 76
FY2004, 2, 10, 19, 20, 62, 64, 65, 71, 74, 75, 81, 82
FY2004 National Defense Authorization Act, 2, 19, 63, 71, 81

## G

gender, 16
General Accounting Office, GAO, 17, 39, 53, 55, 109
General Schedule, GS, 8, 9, 13, 16
GI Bill, 4
Great Depression, 18

## H

health care, 2, 6, 7, 15-18, 23-35, 37-41, 43-47, 50-52, 54, 56
health care benefits, 39
Health Care Financing Administration, HCFA, 50

Health Maintenance Organization, HMO, 25, 43, 55,
housing, 1, 2, 6, 7, 9, 15, 18, 66

## I

inflation, 12, 40, 71-73
Iraq war, 1-4, 19, 81

## L

labor market, 3, 17, 107
living standards, 1, 4, 7
Lord v. United States, 28

## M

mandatory retirement provisions, 99, 101, 102
Manhatten General Equip. Co. V. Commissioner, 28
Manpower and Personnel Subcommittee, 17
Marine Corps, 29, 40, 86, 88, 104
Medicare, 25-27, 32-34, 38, 39, 42, 44, 46-56
Medicare+Choice, 52
Memorandum of Agreement, 106
Memorandum of Understanding, MOU, 105, 107, 108, 111
military compensation, 2, 5-7, 10, 15, 17-19, 69, 81
military culture, 7
military families, 4
Military Health Services System, 37-40
military retirees, 18, 23, 25-27, 30-35, 37-39, 43, 44, 50-53, 56, 61-64, 68, 75, 77, 78, 81, 83
Military Retirement Fund, 73, 74
Military Retirement Reform Act of 1986, 19, 65, 71
military retirement system, 74
military technicians, 85-91, 99, 101, 105, 107, 109, 112, 113
military treatment facilities, MTFs, 24, 26, 27, 53, 55
Montgomery GI Bill, 4, 6
moral obligation, 31-33, 47, 90, 113

# Index

## N

national defense, 3
National Defense Act of 1916, 87, 103, 105
National Defense Authorization Act, 2, 11-14, 19, 24, 25, 28, 31, 32, 35, 47, 62, 63, 65, 67, 68, 71, 72, 76, 78, 81, 82, 85, 89, 90-92, 96, 103, 111, 112
National Defense Authorization Act for Fiscal Year 1998, 89, 112
National Guard, 22, 80, 85-91, 103, 105, 106, 109, 112, 113
National Guard Technicians Act, NDAA, 2, 11, 19, 20, 87, 105, 106
National Guard Technicians Act in 1968, 109
Navy, 22, 27, 29, 34, 39, 40, 70, 86
non-availability statement, 43
non-dual-status technicians, 87-91, 93, 96-102, 109, 111-113

## O

Office of Management and Budget, OMB, 59, 82
Operation Enduring Freedom, 20

## P

pay gap, 2, 14, 16, 17
pay grades, 5, 11, 15, 16
pay raises, 1-3, 5, 9, 10, 14
"pay table reform", 5
Pentagon, 29
permanent change of station, PCS, 6
pharmaceuticals, 48, 55, 56
post-Cold War, 4
Preferred Provider Organization, PPO, 25
pre-Redux system, 65, 66
private sector, 14-17, 46, 74, 98, 101

## R

recruiting, 1-7, 17-19, 24, 26-28, 33, 47, 63, 69
Redux formula, 67, 72
"Redux" system, 19
Regular Military Compensation, 7, 66

retention, 1-7, 19, 27, 69
Retired Officers Association, 26, 27
retired pay, 1, 2, 6, 7, 16, 19, 20, 45, 58, 61, 62, 64-81, 83, 84, 92, 99, 102
retirement, 1, 6, 16, 17, 19, 20, 27, 38, 58, 61, 63-71, 73-77, 80, 84-86, 89-92, 97-103, 113

## S

Selected Reserve, 20, 86-88, 92, 99, 102, 110-112
September 11, 2001, 1, 4, 5, 64, 69
Social Security, 46, 50, 58, 59, 68
social security benefits, 68
special compensation, 76-82
standard of living, 3
"stop-loss" restrictions, 4
Supreme Court, 29
Survivor Benefit Plan, 20
survivor benefits, 61

## T

telemedicine, 42
Temporary Early Retirement Authority, 68, 78
terrorism, 4, 5
Tricare benefit plan, 24
Tricare for Life, 35, 38, 44, 47, 48, 50, 52
Tricare Prime, 25, 38, 41, 43, 45, 48, 55
Tricare Prime Remote, 38
TRICARE program, 18
Tricare Senior Prime, 48
Tricare Senior Supplement Demonstration Program, 49
Tricare Standard, 25, 38, 41, 43, 44, 55
20-year retirement, 69

## U

unemployment, 3-5, 18
unfunded liability, 73, 74
unreduced annuity, 85, 92-97, 99

## V

Veterans Administration, VA, 22, 46, 57-59, 61, 62, 75-79, 83, 84

VA disability compensation, 61, 62, 75, 76, 77, 79, 83, 84
veterans' pensions, 57

## W

Warsaw Pact, 42

World War II, 57, 63

## Y

years-of-service, 9